William Romaine

Discourses Upon Solomon's Song

Preached at St. Dunstan's church, in the West, London

William Romaine

Discourses Upon Solomon's Song
Preached at St. Dunstan's church, in the West, London

ISBN/EAN: 9783337318536

Printed in Europe, USA, Canada, Australia, Japan

Cover: Foto ©Lupo / pixelio.de

More available books at **www.hansebooks.com**

DISCOURSES

UPON

Solomon's Song.

PREACHED AT

St. DUNSTAN's CHURCH, in the WEST,
L O N D O N.

By W. ROMAINE, *M. A.*
LECTURER OF THE SAID CHURCH.

A NEW EDITION,
REVISED BY THE AUTHOR.

WE HAVE KNOWN AND BELIEVED THE LOVE THAT GOD HATH TO US. GOD IS LOVE; AND HE THAT DWELLETH IN LOVE, DWELLETH IN GOD, AND GOD IN HIM.—1 JOHN iv. 16.

L O N D O N:
Printed by *T. CHAPMAN.*
Sold by H. TRAPP, Paternoster-Row, and
J. PRIDDON, Fleet-Street.
1789.

TO THE
PARISHIONERS
OF
St. DUNSTAN's IN THE WEST.

My dear Brethren,

I TAKE this opportunity of acknowledging the many and great favours which I have received from you. My gratitude cannot better appear, than in labouring to the beſt of my power in that ſtation to which you have called me. Ever ſince you were pleaſed unanimouſly to chooſe me your Lecturer, I have endeavoured to diſcharge my duty as one who muſt give an account; and in what manner I diſcharge it, let theſe Sermons, which I now dedicate unto you, bear witneſs. There is a great and awful day at hand,

hand, in which the righteous scarcely shall be saved, and where then shall the wicked and ungodly appear? On this day at the bar of the almighty Judge I must stand to give an account of my ministry among you: knowing therefore the terror of the Lord, I have not shunned to declare unto you the whole counsel of God. He knoweth my heart, and he has seen how honestly I have preached the word, and how earnest I have been with him in prayer for a blessing upon it. Oh that I may deliver my own soul! And God grant you may deliver yours. You have heard me for some years, and chiefly upon the same subject. I hope you are not tired of hearing of the love of Jesus to poor helpless sinners; I am sure I am not tired of speaking upon it. The first Sermon I preached among you was upon this text, 1 *Cor.* ii. 1, 2. " And I, brethren, when I came to " you, came not with excellency of speech, " or of wisdom, declaring unto you the testi- " mony of God: for I determined not to " know any thing among you, save Jesus " Christ, and him crucified." What I then determined

determined in God's strength, I have thus far been enabled to perform. The great subject of all my preaching, as ye know, is Christ Jesus the Lord, inviting and calling careless sinners from the error of their ways, and pressing them to come to Christ for the pardon of their sins, for strength to subdue sin, and for grace to do good works pleasant and acceptable unto God. This pardon, strength and grace are not to be had, but from Christ. He alone has them to give; and that you might see the necessity of applying to him for them, I have been continually setting forth the misery of fallen man, until he receives Christ Jesus the Lord for his Saviour and his God, and the complete happiness he enjoys after he has received him. With what success I have preached you must give an account at the same awful bar, at which I am to be tried, and before a judge who is no respecter of persons. Oh that I may not appear against any of you in that great day. I have good reason to believe that many of you will then be, I pray God you may all then be, my joy and crown of rejoicing. Happy will it be for you and me, if I should see the judge place you all on his right hand. And whether you was brought to this blessedness by my ministry or not, if you do but enjoy it, I shall have cause to glorify God on your behalf.

My brethren, the time is short. Work while it is day: for the night cometh, in which no man can work. It is but a short day, in which you have to finish the work of eternity; therefore give all diligence to make your calling and election sure. Get possession and enjoyment of the present graces of salvation, without which you cannot have any well-grounded hopes of eternal salvation. Jesus must save you from the guilt, and save you from the dominion of sin, he must justify you by his righteousness, and sanctify you by his spirit, before you can see the face of God with joy in his kingdom of glory. And have you then received these graces from him? This, my beloved brethren, is the most interesting question

question you can put to yourselves. Upon the decision of it depends an eternity of happiness or misery. Have you received these graces, or not? May he, that teacheth man wisdom, teach you to answer it to yourselves, as you will answer it to him. May he lead you into all truth. Save you from all sin. Enable you to live to his glory, and make you happy in his love here in time and in eternity.

God knoweth, that this is the prayer of my heart. When that solemn day shall come, in which all secrets shall be laid open, then it will be known with what view I have written this Dedication. God grant my design in it may be answered, and may it then appear that you have reaped the profit from it which I most heartily desired. Having taken this occasion of thanking you for all temporal favours, my love to your souls would not let me lose an opportunity of speaking a word for Christ, although it was out of the pulpit. He has unsearchable, inestimable and eternal riches

riches in his power, and to persuade you to seek them has been and shall be the labour, and to intreat him to bestow them upon you, shall be the prayer, of

Your faithful Minister and

Servant in the Lord Jesus,

William Romaine.

PREFACE.

Reader,

I Here offer thee a Volume of Sermons upon some parts of the Song of Songs. They were composed and preached at a time, when I had some thoughts of treating the whole book in a plain practical way; but that design being laid aside, I have made some of the Sermons public, hoping they may be the means of removing men's prejudices, and of reconciling their minds to this sweet portion of God's holy word.

It is a certain, but a melancholy matter of fact, that there has been more ridicule wasted upon the Song, than upon any other portion of God's word. And we need not marvel at it. The devil has a particular spite against this book; he hates the subject, and he hates the composition. He cannot bear to hear of man's being restored to that fellowship and communion with God which himself once had, but can never hope for again: and therefore this treatise upon it is the object of his most devilish malice,

malice, and he is always stirring up his agents to write and to speak contemptibly of it. And he has been too successful in his temptation. Many persons fell into it, because it flattered their pride. They set up themselves for judges of all subjects, divine as well as human, and made their reason the criterion of all truth. They tried this book by their reason, and they did not understand it, therefore they thought no body did. Upon the force of this conclusion they took a general licence to ridicule it; but the conclusion is not logical: for certainly the book may be intelligible, although they do not understand it. Modest reason would incline them to be of this opinion, because many learned men in every age have thought it intelligible, and many good men without much learning have understood it. The true cause of which was this: They understood the subject treated of in this book, which the enemies of it did not. A deaf man is as good a judge of a fine piece of music, as a man who has no real heart-love for God is of a treatise upon the love of God: for as he has no knowledge of the subject, how can he understand what is written upon it? If a man ignorant of mathematics was to take up Sir Isaac Newton's Principia, *and to cry out,* What stuff is this? Who can make any thing

thing of these strange lines and figures, and these *A*'s and *B*'s? A great mathematician standing by would pity the poor man's ignorance. In like manner when any person takes up a book upon communion with God, and either does not believe there is such a thing, or has had no experience of it, how can he understand what is written? It must appear to him mere jargon and gibberish; and if he has a talent at ridicule, here is a tempting occasion for him to display it. Whereas the fault is not in the book, but in the man who reads it. It may be a perfect composition, and he may be no judge of it. The book is plain enough to them who are properly qualified to read it. If you understand the true genius of the tongue in which it is written, and have some insight into the subject of which it treats, it will then be as intelligible as any other portion of scripture; but the enemies of this book understand neither of these particulars. They are not qualified to judge, and yet they venture to condemn it: for

First, They are not acquainted with the nature of the Hebrew tongue, without which no man should pretend to be a critic upon the writings of the Old Testament. If any person should

should write professedly against Homer, *and try to prove there was no genius, invention, or sublimity in his poems, with what contempt would the learned treat his performance, especially if they knew that this ignoramus did not understand one word of* Greek, *no nor one letter. If such an attack upon* Homer *appear ridiculous to men of learning, how much more ridiculous should an attack of the some nature appear upon a treatise in* Hebrew: *because the* Hebrew *is more difficult to be translated word for word, than any* Greek *author can be. It has some peculiar properties and idioms, which no other language has, with which every critic should be acquainted, lest he should raise objections that would only betray his own ignorance. The* Hebrew *is a fixt language. It is not like ours, arbitrary and changeable. We are continually gaining some new word, or dropping some obsolete one, or affixing some new idea to a word, which we have done remarkably in the word* charity. *When our liturgy was compiled, and afterwards when the present translation of the Bible was made, charity signified love, but now we use it for nothing but giving of alms. If you were to use it in its ancient sense, and to talk of the charity of God, who would not be understood.*

But

PREFACE.

But the Hebrew *is free from these imperfections. It is fixt in nature, and cannot change unless nature should. Every word stands for some material and sensible object, which God created to represent and to give us ideas of some correspondent and spiritual object. Like as in parables there is an outward and literal sense, by which an inward and spiritual meaning is conveyed, so is it in every* Hebrew *word. And a critic should understand* Hebrew *upon this plan. He should be acquainted with the genius of the* Hebrew *tongue, and with its manner of expressing spiritual things under their appointed images in nature. And it is more necessary he should have this knowledge in order to understand this book, because it is the worst translated of all scripture. Our translators have not failed more in any part of the* Old Testament, *than they have here. Instead of giving us the spiritual meaning of the words, they have seldom given us any thing but the literal sense, and sometimes they have given us the* Hebrew *word without any translation at all. If they had translated the prophecy of* Isaiah *in the same injudicious manner, it would have been as abstruse as this book is. I hope to see it made as intelligible as the prophecy of* Isaiah. *There are several persons*

persons at present in our church of great leisure and great abilities, and it is much to be wished they would employ them in explaining this book. The most proper method they could take seems to me, to settle first the true literal sense of every word in the Song, and then, as it is entirely a spiritual book treating of communion with God, to fix the spiritual idea to each word; and where we have not a proper word in English *to express the full sense of a* Hebrew *word, they might give it in a short paraphrase. Whenever this is done the mouths of our ignorant mockers will be stopped, and it will appear that all their objections arose from their ignorance.*

Thus the enemies of this book are ignorant of the true genius of the Hebrew *tongue, in which it is written, and they borrow their arguments against it not from the faults of the book itself, but from the faults in the translation; and they are also ignorant of the subject upon which it treats. It is one of the deep things of God, which the natural man cannot understand. He has none of this love to God which is here described, nor can he attain it by any means in his own power. It is a love that comes down from God. He is*

the

the giver of it, and it is shed abroad in the heart by the Holy Spirit, who bestows the comforts of it upon them, that are pardoned and reconciled to the Father in the Son of his love, and that can therefore truly say with the apostle John—" *We know and have believed* " *the love that God hath to us.*" *Whoever sits down to read this book, be he ever so learned in other matters, yet if he has no knowledge of God's love to him, he cannot understand what he reads. The objectors to this book are so far from pretending to have any of this experimental love of God, that they laugh at it and ridicule it; whereby they plainly declare, that they are not judges of the subject upon which this book treats, and therefore they are not fit to sit in judgment upon it.*

These are the two principal reasons why this book is so little understood, and so much ridiculed. I need not enlarge upon them here, because they are often taken notice of in the Sermons, to which I refer the reader. When I first thought of making them public, I did not foresee how seasonable they would be. It appears to me quite providential, that these Sermons upon the love of God should be published just at this time, when I am furiously attacked
by

by a nameless writer, and charged with preaching nothing but hell and damnation. It would have been as true a charge, if he had said I always preached in Hebrew. *This volume shall answer for me. Here my doctrine is, Believe and thou shalt be saved, love God and thou shalt be happy. May he who has this saving belief, and this happy love to give, for his mercy's sake bestow them upon this my bitter enemy and open persecutor.*

I have nothing more to add, but to intreat the blesser of all nations to accompany the reading of these Sermons with his blessing. May he water them with the dew of his heavenly grace, and render them useful and profitable to every person into whose hands they may fall. Reader, if thou findest any unction from the Holy One in them, and reapest any benefit from them, give God the glory, and pray for the author. Thou canst not do me any service which I more want or value than thy prayers. Pray, that the grace of Christ may do more in me, and that I may do more for Christ. And in return I will pray for thee, that the Spirit of the living God may enable thee to understand this divine Song, and to experience the comforts of its doctrine, and then thou wilt

wilt be in poſſeſſion of the greateſt happineſs thou canſt enjoy on this ſide of heaven.

Upon reviſing theſe ſheets for a new edition of the following Sermons, I had great reaſon to bleſs the Lord God, that my views of this ſubject were the ſame as they were ſeveral years ago—only confirmed by long experience. It is a good thing to be eſtabliſhed in the truth, and by conſtant uſe to get into holy and happy practice. When the believer has received Chriſt, it is his privilege to be growing up into him in all things. Flouriſhing like the palm tree, and mounting up like the cedar in Lebanon. Certain doctrines are then not to be diſputed. The eſſential glory of Immanuel—The abſolute perfection of his ſaving work—The effectual application of it to the conſciences, to the hearts, and to the lives of believers by the Holy Spirit; in theſe it is good and right that there ſhould be no variableneſs nor ſhadow of turning. Jeſus Chriſt, and his work, and his Spirit, and his fulneſs, being the ſame, yeſterday, to day, and for ever.

Much has been written and ſpoken againſt theſe Sermons, as if I had therein made too much of Chriſt. I think it impoſſible. His perſon is above all bleſſing and praiſe. His ſalvation

tion is infinitely perfect, and contains an eternal fulness of all graces and glories. His promises are exceeding great, and exceeding precious—already made good to him, as the head, and by him made good to all his people. When the spirit of life that is in him sets them free from the law of sin and of death, they are pardoned, and righteous, and holy, and blessed in the Beloved. Which of them can come up to the greatness of such a subject? Who can shew forth all the praises of such a Jesus? I cannot. Instead of thinking that I have spoken too highly of him, I am very sensible of my many and great failings. May the glorifier of Jesus enable me to speak more worthily of him in earth and heaven.

DISCOURSES

UPON THE

SONG *of* SOLOMON.

SERMON I.

Chap. i. Ver. 1.

The Song of Songs which is Solomon's.

GOD is love. The whole scripture is a history of the wonders which his love has done for the children of men. It was love which first gave being to the universe. The same continued love has preserved it. But the description of the works of creation and preservation takes up a small part of the sacred volume. The great subject of it is redeeming love. In this sweet and amiable light God has proposed himself to our consideration. When his justice was offended at the transgression of his holy law, his love contrived how to get glory to every divine attribute, by pardoning and saving the transgressor. He had provided the covenant of grace, in which was the richest display of his infinite love. In this covenant he glories. He sets it forth and recommends it, as the greatest work of God, and has revealed the *Old Testament* and the *New* to demonstrate to sinners, that our redeeming God is love. When *Moses* desired to see his glory, he did not refer him to the works of creation, or to the instances which he had seen of his almighty power; but he sent him to the mercies of redemption, in which he might have the strongest evidences of God's glory. He proclaimed himself as the *Old Testament* God, under the stile and title of—" The Lord, " the Lord God, merciful and gracious, " long suffering, and abundant in goodness " and truth, keeping mercy for thousands, for- " giving iniquity and transgression and sin." (*Exod.* xxxiv. 6, 7.) This description was fulfilled, when the brightness of divine glory was revealed in the person of Jesus Christ. When he came into the world to save men from their sins, then his disciples beheld his glory, and believed that God was love: then they saw the completion of what was written

in

in all the scriptures, more especially in the *Song of Songs*, concerning the greatness of redeeming love: for though all scripture treats largely of it, yet this is an entire treatise upon the subject. It contains a lively description of the perfect love which our redeeming God has for returning sinners, and of the grateful affection which his love stirs up in them. He relates what graces and blessings he would bestow upon them, and they express their happiness in the enjoyment of his graces and blessings. He finds them black and deformed sinners, and he presents them fair and without spot in the sight of God, and they, knowing him to be *their* beloved and *their* friend, see him altogether lovely. Upon this subject they discourse, setting forth the happiness of their mutual love

The *Jews* call this book " The Holy of " Holies," and so it is to every one, who has the love of God shed abroad in his heart. Here he converses with the most holy persons and things, and has a foretaste of those pleasures which are at God's right-hand for evermore. But here the carnal and unregenerate man reads at the peril of his own soul.

foul. He enters as it were into the holy of holies, which was death by the law. He is ignorant of God's being in this place. He puts not off his shoe, although it be holy ground. He puts not off concerning his former conversation the old man, who is corrupt according to the deceitful lusts, and who neither does understand the things of God treated of in this book, nor can understand them for want of a spiritual discernment. He cannot know them, says the word of truth, because they are spiritually discerned; and therefore if he meddle with them he must prophane them. The more sacred they are, the more contrary are they to his nature. The more wholsome they are to the spiritual man, the more poison will the natural man extract from them; and that which is a favour of life, proves to him a favour of death,

Away then ye prophane. Come not near to the holy of holies, nor presume to look into it, lest ye die. You are no more fit to read this book, than you are to partake of the sacred elements at the Lord's table. With your carnal unregenerate heart you will read the one, and partake of the other to your greater condemnation. Oh keep back then, and presume not to look

look into, or to judge of the sacred mysteries of this divine song. But if you will venture to read it, and to ridicule it, remember that it is one of the treasures of divine wisdom; and though you may level your wit against a Song of *Solomon's*, yet it falls upon the Almighty God who inspired it. And are you arrived at such desperate wit, as to break jests upon God, and to make sport with his omnipotence? Oh fear and tremble for yourselves, lest while you are shooting up your arrows, even your bitter words against heaven, God should send them back upon your own heads with a swift destruction. May his grace shew you your danger, and dispose you to leave your sins; and whenever you are stirred up to seek pardon and peace in Christ Jesus, then you will begin to understand this book; and when you have any experience of God's love to you, then you will find comfort and profit in reading it.

I propose through God's assistance to treat of some parts of it in a practical way, and to make our future consideration of these particular passages more plain and easy, I shall at present lay before you a general plan of the book. And this we have in the words now read.

read. They are the title prefixed to it by its divine author, and serve as a short comment to explain its principal use. I shall therefore endeavour,

First, To settle the true sense and meaning of the words—From whence we may gather,

Secondly, That the scope and design of this sweet portion of scripture is to describe the mutual love of Christ and his church.

Thirdly, I shall bring some arguments to prove, that this is the scope and design of it. And,

Lastly, I will reduce these truths to practice, and make some useful inferences from them.

And *First*, The words now read are the title, which the Holy Spirit prefixed to the book, that they might serve as a key to open its scope and design. The Song of Songs which is concerning *Solomon*, which treats of *Solomon*. A song in the scripture usage of the term, consists in setting forth the praises of God.

It

It is a hymn to his honour and glory. The fpiritual fongs of fcripture have no other object but the God of love, and no other end but to raife and to exalt our ideas of him, and of his works, efpecially of his works of grace, whereby he brings loft finners to an happy fence and fweet experience of his love. St. *Paul* has given us a fhort, but it is a very full comment upon the fcripture fongs (*Col.* iii. 16.) " Let the word of Chrift dwell in
" you richly in all wifdom, teaching and
" admonifhing one another in pfalms, and
" hymns, and fpiritual fongs, finging with
" grace in your hearts unto the Lord."
Hence we learn the nature of thefe fongs; they are the words of Chrift, reavealed by him and concerning him, and in them we are to teach and to admonifh one another, to the end that the word of Chrift may dwell in us richly in all wifdom: for they are fpiritual fongs; and he that fings them muft have grace in his heart, without this qualification he will fing the fong of fools; and he muft alfo fing " to the Lord," to the glory and honour of his holy name. After this apoftolical rule we may explain this fong. It is the word of Chrift, revealed by him, and concerning him, and we are to teach and to admonifh

one

one another in the things of Christ out of this song. We have the apostle's command to do it, with this encouragement, that the word of Christ may dwell in us richly in all wisdom: for this song is of a spiritual nature, treating of spiritual persons and things, and cannot be sung aright unless grace be in the heart, nor with profit, unless we have an eye to the Lord in every word of it. If we look off from him to any lower object, we not only lose sight of its scope and design, but we also form a judgment of it contrary to the judgment of the Holy Spirit, who has exalted this above the rest of the scripture songs, and has dignified it with the high title of " The Song of Songs." There are many divine songs, but this is by way of eminence above, and in copiousness comprehends, them all. It is the sum and substance of them, and the point to which they tend. God is the subject of every spiritual song, and what can we find in God which calls for louder songs of praise, than that love which is above all his works; which was before them, for it gave them their being, which is with them to preserve it, and will be with them to the boundless ages of eternity. Surely a hymn upon this exalted

subject

subject deserves the title of " The Song of " Songs;" especially when the divine person, of whom he treats, is considered in it under his most amiable character, and set forth under the stile and title of the prince of peace; for this is the meaning of the word *Solomon* in *Hebrew*. *The Song of Songs which is* Solomon's, our translation reads; but the *Hebrew* particle put before *Solomon* is the sign not of the genetive, but of the dative case, and is frequently rendered concerning or touching such a person or thing. Thus, *Isaiah* v. 1. Now will I sing to my well-beloved a song of my beloved, *touching* his vineyard. And again, *Psalm* xlv. 1. I speak of the things which I have made *touching* the king. It is also several times rendered *concerning*, as Gen. xix. 21. I have accepted thee *concerning* this thing; and in *Jer.* xlix. it is frequently translated *concerning*. In this sense it is here used. The Song of Songs which is concerning *Solomon* — not king Solomon, but the prince of peace, Jesus Christ, of whom *Solomon* was a type and figure, as it appears from the lxxiid *Psalm*, which has the same title with the Song. It is inscribed to *Solomon* — Is concerning him, and treats of him; but several passages of it

can

can be applied to none but Jesus the prince of peace, of whom only it could be truly said that he had dominion from one end of the earth to the other, that all kings should fall down before him, and all nations should serve him, that he should save the souls of the needy, and should redeem their souls, and that prayer should be made unto him continually, and all nations should call him blessed. These things cannot be spoken of king *Solomon* — but they are strictly true of the prince of peace, Jesus the Lord of life and redeemer of sinners. — Therefore the title of the lxxiid *Psalm* has the same meaning with the title of the *Song*; and when the Holy Spirit says, " The Song of Songs which " is concerning the Lord and giver of peace," he would plainly point out to us the principal use of this scripture. It is a treatise concerning the God of love, under the character of the prince of peace, describing how happy we are in Christ Jesus, when we, who sometimes were far off, are made nigh by the blood of Christ: for he is our peace. And this leads me to consider,

Secondly, The scope and design of this sweet portion of scripture. It is to describe
the

the peace, which Chrift has given to the faithful foul, and fets forth the happinefs of the foul in the enjoyment of it. Chriftian peace is the fruit of that love which the Holy Spirit has manifefted to finners, and flows from a fence of their reconciliation with God through Jefus Chrift their Lord, of which the apoftle thus fpeaks: " Being jufti-
" fied by faith we have peace with God
" through our Lord Jefus Chrift, and re-
" joice in hope of the glory of God." And when we have thus tafted how gracious the Lord is, then we cannot but love him, who firft loved us, and the fenfe of this love fills the mind with joy and peace: in this order St. *Paul* has placed thefe graces, " The fruit
" of the Spirit is love, joy, peace." — Our love is by nature placed upon a wrong object. Sin alienated our hearts from God. Our affections are turned from him, and feek for happinefs in creature-comforts. And although daily difappointed, yet they continue to feek it, until the Holy Spirit convince them, that they are feeking happinefs in a vain fhadow, and difquieting themfelves in vain. And when he has fhewn them that neverthelefs they may be compleatly happy in God the Saviour, and has ftirred them up

earneftly

earnestly to desire his salvation, then he has prepared them to read this divine treatise with profit: the scope and design of which is to set before us Jesus Christ as the only excellent and lovely object of our affections; and when we by the eye of faith behold him, and by the power of faith are united to him, then we know what the apostle meant when he said, " To them that be-" lieve Jesus is precious ;" and we can take up the words of the believer in the *Song* and declare, that he is altogether lovely, the chiefest among ten thousand. And thus every other object will fade away in our esteem, and grow mean and worthless in comparison of God our Saviour; whereby we shall be able to enter into the spirit of the song. We shall know something of that spiritual fellowship and communion of which it treats: for it dwells largely upon the mutual joys, and mutual praises of Christ and the believing soul, describing the complete happiness which they have in each other. This is the general plan of the book, which is very well expressed in the argument put before it, in the Bible that was in use in queen *Elziabeth's* time — " In this Song " *Solomon*, by most sweet and comfortable
" allegories

"allegories and parables, describeth the per-
"fect love of Jesus Christ, the true *Solomon*
"and king of peace, and the faithful of his
"church, which he hath sanctified, and ap-
"pointed to be his spouse, holy, chaste, and
"without reprehension. So that here is de-
"clared the singular love of the bridegroom
"toward the bride, and his great and excel-
"lent benefits wherewith he doth enrich
"her of his pure bounty and grace, without
"any of her deservings. Also the earnest
"affection of the church, which is inflamed
"with the love of Christ, desiring to be
"more and more joined to him in love, and
"not to be forsaken for any spot or blemish
"that is in her."

This was the judgment of our reformers—and they were not singular in it, as I propose to shew under my *Third* head, which was, To bring some arguments to prove, that this is the scope and design of the book.

The first argument, which would occur to every serious person, is the universal consent of expositers. All the *Jewish* writers suppose it to treat of the spiritual union between

tween Chrift and the believer. All chriftian writers underftand it in the fame fenfe. And the unanimous opinion of all learned and good men ought certainly to have great weight with us: for the fcope and defign of the book muft be very plain and clear, fince there never was any difpute about it in the church of God. This then being the re-received fenfe, I may proceed to examine upon what principles it came to be fo univerfally received. I fuppofe men were led to confider it in this light from the eftablifhed method of explaining fcripture; and this is the fecond argument I fhall ufe.

The fcriptures are fuited to man in his prefent ftate. While he is here in the body he cannot converfe immediately with fpiritual objects: he can only fee them comparatively, as compared to and illuftrated by material and fenfible objects. The fcriptures take this method of inftruction. They teach us fpiritual and heavenly things under their expreffive images in nature. Whoever confidered the fcriptures in this light, could not reft in the literal fenfe of the *Song*. He knew that all fcripture had a fpiritual fenfe, and therefore in reading the *Song* he would
confider

confider what the fpiritual fenfe could be, and he could not eafily miftake it, when he recollected what was the one great end and aim of all fcripture. Every part of it was to lead men to fome knowledge of Chrift, which is the *third* argument tending to open to us the fcope and defign of this divine book.

Search the fcriptures, fays he of whom they write, for thefe are they which teftify of me — The *Song* is part of thefe fcriptures, and therefore it teftifies of Chrift; and what other teftimony does it bear of him, than in fetting forth the love which he has for his faithful people?

The teftimony of Jefus, fays St. *John*, is the fpirit of prophecy. If you underftand the prophetical fpirit of this book, you will read in it the teftimony of Jefus: therefore if yon don't fee how it bears teftimony to him, you have no infight into its prophetical fpirit.

Again we read, " That the holy fcriptures " are able to make a man wife unto falva- " tion, through faith which is in Chrift Je- " fus; for all fcripture is given by infpira- " tion

"tion of God." (2 *Tim.* iii. 15, 16.) From whence I infer, that the *Song* being part of scripture, is given by inspiration of God, and was therefore given, that it might make the man of God wise unto salvation, and this it does by establishing him in the faith, which is in Christ Jesus.

Another proof may be taken from the xlvth *Psalm*, which is a song of loves. The subject and the manner of the composition are the same with this divine book. They treat of the love of Christ to his church, and after the manner of a dialogue, and the xlvth *Psalm* is applied to Christ by an infallible interpreter. St. *Paul* in the 1st of the *Hebrews* and the 8th verse says, that it was written of God the Son: from whence we may conclude, that the *Song* being upon the same subject, and drawn up in the same manner, treats also of the love of God the Son to his faithful people. And to confirm the interpretation of these more general proofs, I may mention a fourth argument, taken from those places of scripture wherein Christ is spoken of in the very terms used in the *Song*. The scripture often speaks of him under the character of the bridegroom. In the

the 25th of St *Matthew* we have the parable of the ten virgins who went out to meet the bridegroom, who in the 13th verse is called the son of man. In the 5th of the *Ephesians*, St. *Paul* is treating of the love and union between husbands and wives, and in the 32d verse he says, " This is a great mys-
" tery, but I speak concerning Christ and his
" church," in the same manner, and with the same expressions, which are used in the song, and which are carried on through the *New Testament :* for thus we read in one of the last scenes of the *Revelation* of St. *John*, that the multitude of the heavenly host cried aloud as the voice of mighty thunderings, saying, Hallelujah, for the Lord God omnipotent reigneth, let us be glad and rejoice and give honour unto him: for the marriage of the lamb is come, and his wife hath made herself ready. And in the 21st chapter St. *John* informs us who the bride the lamb's wife is, the church, the *Jerusalem* that is above, which is the spiritual mother of us all, even of every one of us who shall be so happy as to be called to the marriage-supper of the lamb.

From these authorities it appears to me undeniably evident, that it is common in scripture to speak of Christ in the very same manner that he is spoken of in the *Song*; and therefore summing up all these arguments together, considering that the expositors, *Jews* and Christians, are agreed about the plan and design of it, and that the received sense is agreeable to the general rule for interpreting scripture, and is founded upon clear reasoning from many particular passages, and more especially from those passages wherein express mention is made of Christ's love to the faithful, under the very images used to represent it in the *Song*, we may certainly from hence conclude, that the scope and design of this sweet portion of scripture is to set forth in the most lively and affecting manner the mutual joys and mutual praises of Christ, and the faithful.

Having thus far endeavoured to settle and establish the principal use of this sacred book, I come in the *fourth* and *last* place to reduce what has been said into practice, and to draw some useful inferences from it.

The *Song*, as you have heard, is of the nature of a parable, wherein spiritual things are described by material. It is one of the offices of the wisdom that is from above, to understand a parable a parable and the interpretation thereof. I have endeavoured to give you the interpretation of one of the sweetest of all the divine parables. And are there any of you, my brethren, who after what has been said are not yet reconciled to this book? Do you think, that it had better have been left out of the sacred volume? Consider, that your opinion weighs nothing against the unanimous consent of the church of God, and your opinion is fouded upon your ignorance of the things of God. If you understood this book, you could not think meanly of it; but in order to understand it, you must have some experience of that love of which it treats — having never tasted of it, you cannot enter into the spirit of the descriptions of it here made by Christ and by the faithful. Instead then of looking into the book for matter of censure, look into your own hearts, and beg of God to shew you how much you stand in need of having the love of Christ shed abroad in them; and whenever he enables you to say with the apostle, Jesus Christ loved me and gave himself for me, then you will taste and see how exceedingly sweet every image and description is in this divine song.

If you cannot be perfuaded to defire the love of God may be fhed abroad in your hearts, you will entertain a mean opinion of this treatife upon it. But for the fake of your dear and immortal foul, fuffer not yourfelf to fpeak irreverently of it. If God ever revealed himfelf to man, this is part of his revelation. The holy and eternal Spirit, who infpired all fcripture, fpake this by his unerring wifdom. He is the author, and the fubject is the deep things of God. Let not then a difrefpectful word come out of your mouth againft it. But if you will fuffer your wit to run into licentioufnefs, remember that you ridicule this book at the peril of your foul. You are guilty of blafphemy againft the Moft High. And how can you think it fafe, to jeft upon the Almighty, and to make fport with his omnipotence? Why will you fet God at defiance, and add frefh fuel to his wrath, as if all your other fins would not fink you deep enough into the pit of deftruction? If you have any love left for your eternal intereft, forbear this defperate wit; and beg of God to enlighten the darknefs of your underftanding, that you may fee the fcope and defign of this facred fong. And to thofe perfons who defire this, I make my fecond remark.

You

You do not clearly comprehend the things written in this book, but you defire to comprehend them. If this defire be from God, it will put you upon praying for the experience of that love, which is here treated of. You may poffibly come at the meaning of fome things in it, but you cannot know them practically nor profitably, until you are taught them of God. You cannot tell what the love of God is, until it be fhed abroad in your heart. No defcription can make you acquainted with it; and therefore look up to God who has it to give. Afk him out of the riches of his grace to beftow it upon you; and when he gives you the comfortable fenfe of it, then you will have the beft key to open the myfteries of this divine fong. And for your encouragement in feeking, remember that this love is free. Though it be ineftimable, yet it is to be had without money and without price. God had no motive to fhew it to finners but his own inherent mercy, and he waits for no merit or qualification in them: for it is to fupply the want of all merit and qualification: and he has already begun to beftow the riches of this free love upon you, by making you fenfible of your want of it, and by putting you upon feeking for it. Wait upon him then in the ways of his ordinances, and he will finish what he has begun. He will enable you to love him, because he first loved you. Ask this out of a due sense of your unworthiness, and the Father for the sake of his Son will shed abroad his love in your hearts by the Holy Ghost. And thus he will bring you into the happy number of those believers, to whom I make my third and last inference.

You, my christian brethren, can read this sweet portion of scripture with delight and profit. You know it to be true by your own experience. You look upon Jesus Christ in the light here described: for he is your peace, and you find his dealings with your souls are the very same which the *Song* mentions. For what the *Song* says of the church in general, must be true of every individual who is a member of it— For the church is nothing more than a congregation of believers united by faith and by the bond of the spirit to Christ the head of the spiritual body, and by love to one another— United to him, as the members are to the head, and united to one another as the members are in the same body. What therefore is spoken in the *Song*

of

of the whole church, as the spouse of Christ, is true of every particular christian. And what is said of the church is briefly this: In the first chapter the church expresses a strong desire for nearer communion with Christ, and then there follows some declining of her affection. After this we have her recovery, a regaining of her first love: and yet she afterwards declines again in her affection, her love grows cold, and she falls into a state of desertion. Christ hides his presence from her more than he did in her former coldness, and this continues, until perceiving Christ's constant affection to her, notwithstanding her unkind treatment of him, she recovers, and follows him more closely, and with a more constant love than before.

These passages agree with the experience of the best christians in the course of their own lives, and therefore the *Song* is not a dark unintelligible book to them. They find it to be an experimental treatise upon the love of Jesus Christ to his people. And all of you, my christian brethren, understand it in this light. You have read it with care, praying the holy inspirer of it to enlighten your understandings, that you might see its true

true sense and spiritual meaning; and he has opened to you the truth of its descriptions. The Holy Spirit has drawn you to Christ, and has made you happy in the sense of his love, and thus he has given you the best comment upon the *Song*. The more he enables you to taste of this love, the more clearly will you understand the *Song*. You will have the greater insight into it, the nearer access you have to the Father, with confidence through the faith that is in Christ: for what is written concerning communion with God must certainly be best understood by those, who live in close communion with him. This is your privilege. Remember how great and high it is, and act worthy of it. You have fellowship with the Father, and with his Son Jesus Christ. The Holy Spirit is the bond of this communion, and therefore it is called the " communion of the Holy Ghost." Oh beware then of every thing that would grieve or offend him. As his is an holy office, entirely relating to holiness, nothing can displease this Holy Spirit so much as sin. He is of purer eyes than to behold the least iniquity. The least thought of sin offends him: for it is sin that pollutes his sacred residence, and defiles the temple of the heart. Sin makes

makes him withdraw and hide the light of his countenance, and with-hold the sweet sense of his comfortable presence. Oh beware then, as you love your own peace of mind, as you love your God and his glory, as you love Jesus Christ and his salvation, beware of the least approach to sin. Pray, watch, strive against it. Resist unto blood striving against sin. Wait upon God in all his ordinances to get power over it. And the more you are dead to sin and alive unto God, the nearer fellowship will you have with the Father, and with his Son Jesus Christ, and as this fellowship is the subject of the *Song*, you will therefore understand it the better, and experience more of its sweetness.

My christian brethren you have tasted of its sweetness. You know the loving kindness of the Lord, and if you would have the constant abiding sense of it, earnestly beseech the Holy Spirit to keep you from offending him in thought, word, and deed. Intreat him to give you grace never to grieve him. Stand in awe, and sin not. Sin is your great enemy. Nothing makes God hide his face from you, but sin. All the darkness and blindness, and depravity, that are in the soul concerning

ing the things of God, come from sin: from it came all misery. Oh watch then and pray always against it. Pray that you may be kept from the works of darkness, and from every error and vice which would cloud the understanding, and hinder your reading this portion of scripture with profit. Look up to the spirit of wisdom, and intreat him to open to you the true sense and meaning of the *Song*, and to give you the happy experience and comforts of its doctrines. And that we may all receive the benefits from it which he intended it should administer to his people, let us humbly ask it of him in the words of our church, which hath taught us to pray, saying,

Blessed Lord, who hast caused *all* holy scriptures (and this portion of them in particular which we have been considering) to be written for our learning; grant that we may in such wise hear them, read, mark, learn, and inwardly digest them, that by patience and comfort of thy holy word, we may embrace, and ever hold fast the blessed hope of everlasting life, which thou hast given us in our Saviour Jesus Christ. *Amen.*

SERMON II.

Chap. i. Ver. 4.

Draw me, we will run after thee.

THE Saviour of sinners is God and man united in one Christ. As God he has all the perfection of heaven, and as man he has all the beauties of this earth; he has every grace of time and every blessing of eternity, which ought to draw and to attract our love. But while men are in their natural unregenerate state, they see none of his perfections and beauties. They behold no form nor comeliness in him, that they should desire him. The world, and the things of it, appear more desireable than he does. The base perishing joys of sense have the entire possession of their affections. Sin is more lovely in their eyes than God the Saviour, and they give up their hearts to its enjoyments in preference to him and his heaven. While they continue to place their love on such unworthy objects, they are incapable of judging of this

this divine fong: for they are not only ftrangers, but alfo enemies to that love, of which it treats; and how then can they fee the beauties of its compofition, or judge of the juftnefs of its fentiments? So long as they love fin, they cannot love Jefus Chrift, and therefore they cannot love the fweet defcriptions in this poem, which fet forth the happinefs of loving him above all things. But when their eyes are opened to fee the exceeding finfulnefs of fin, and their hearts are once drawn from the love of fin; when they have found that it cannot make them happy, then they are glad to hear of a Saviour; and when they have tafted of his love, then they begin to underftand and to admire the beauties of this divine fong, and the more they love him, the greater beauties do they find in it.

The fubject of it is the union between Chrift and the faithful foul. In this all the expofitors of fcripture antient and modern are agreed. It is a fpiritual fong, compofed in the manner of a dialogue. The fpeakers are Chrift, and the believer. The infpirer of it is the Holy and Eternal Spirit, who delivered it by the mouth of *Solomon*. He knew it to be true by his own experience, as every believer does to this day. After he had left God, he fought for happiness in the creatures, but was disappointed. He turned from one object to another, tried the whole circle of worldly enjoyments, and as he past on he wrote upon each *vanity and vexation of spirit*. It pleased God to shew him his error, and to make use of him as a proper person to warn others, from setting their hearts upon any object but God; for if *Solomon* could not find happiness in the world, what can the man do that cometh after the king? This is the subject of the book of *Ecclesiastes*. After *Solomon* had turned from these worldly vanities to serve the living God, he wrote this divine song, to shew what true happiness he had found, and every believer will find, in being united to Christ in the bonds of love and affection. The Holy Spirit had drawn his heart from the love of all inferior objects to God the Redeemer, and had given him faith to see his own interest in what the Redeemer was to do and suffer for him. By these bonds the union was formed and perfected. The Holy Spirit on Christ's part, and faith on the believer's united them to each other. And the believer here describes what happy effects flowed to him

from

from this union, and Chrift defcribes the delight he had in it. The defcriptions of their mutual love and happinefs run through this fong of loves.

The awakened foul begins with expreffing its defire to receive fome fenfible tokens of Chrift's love in the fecond verfe, fetting forth the excellency of it in the third, and at the fame time its own utter inability and infufficiency to attain it, unlefs Chrift would be pleafed to draw the affections from all other objects unto himfelf—*Draw me*, as it follows in the fourth verfe, *and we will run after thee.*—Draw me, Lord Jefus, from the love of the world, and the things of it; draw me from the love of fin and felf. I feel my bondage, I find that I am a flave, and am without ftrength to deliver myfelf. O draw me then by the fweet impulfe of thy good Spirit from my bondage and flavery. And when thou art pleafed to fet my feet at liberty, then *we* will run after thee; *we* in the plural number: for when the heart is once drawn after Chrift, it commands all the faculties, and they which could not ftir before now run, they which had no ftrength now run againft all oppofition, they which
were

were enemies to Chrift, now run after him with joy in the ways of his commandments. Draw me by thy grace, and *we*, every faculty of foul and body, will obey, we will follow the divine attraction, and thou fhalt be our God and king ruling over us, and getting thyfelf glory by fetting up thy kingdom within us. May thefe be the defires of all your hearts. While we are here met together, may the Lord Jefus draw your thoughts from every vain and finful object, and keep them fixed upon this fubject. Oh that he may fend his good Spirit to open your underftandings clearly to fee, and to influence your affections readily to receive,

Firft, The reafons, which induced the awakened finner to defire Chrift would draw him.

Secondly, The fcripture method of drawing the foul unto Chrift.

Thirdly, The certain effects which follow upon its being drawn. And then,

Fourthly, I will reduce thefe particulars to practice, and will apply them clofely, as
God

God shall enable me, to every one of your consciences.

And *First*, We need not look farther than the text for the reasons which induced the awakened sinner to desire Christ would draw him. He found he could not run after Christ, unless he was drawn: for although God be the fountain of all good to his creatures, and the God-man Christ Jesus be the fountain of all good to his sinful creatures, yet they are not willing to go and receive good at his hands. Sin has corrupted all the faculties of the soul, and has turned and alienated them from God; insomuch that they leave God to seek good in the creature, and idolize it by placing their happiness in it. The god of this world, and his riches, and honours, and pleasures have possession of their hearts, and the God of heaven who promises them heavenly riches, and honours, and pleasures, has none of their affections: nay, they hate him. While they love present and sensual gratifications they are haters of God. They hate him, because their sinful nature is opposite to his perfect holiness, and because he has forbidden them these gratifications, which they are determined to enjoy; and they hate him the more, because he he has threatened to punish them, and confcience informs them that they deferve the threatened punishment. This is the ftate of all men by nature. They are lovers of fin, and haters of God, *Rom.* i. 30. And until this hatred be conquered, how can they come to God with any kind of love? Their affections will lead them farther from him every ftep they take, and how can they return, unlefs he draw them to himfelf? If they can but be convinced of the vanity and emptinefs of all thefe creature-comforts, upon which they have fet their hearts, and can fee reafon to think that God will be reconciled and love them, notwithftanding their former oppofition to him, then they will be difpofed to feek his love; but until they be convinced of thefe two truths they cannot be drawn to feek happinefs in God.

This is the plain doctrine of fcripture. Our divine Lord and mafter thus inftructs his difciples (*John* vi. 44.) " No man can " come unto me, except the Father, which " hath fent me draw him." *No man*, be he ever fo moral, civil, and learned, let him have ever fo many natural gifts and acquired accomplifhments, *can come*, has either will or power to come unto me for the graces and blessings which I have to give, *unless the Father which hath sent me draw him*, by the sweet attraction of his good Spirit.

Our church teaches the same doctrine in her tenth article. " The condition of man
" after the fall of *Adam* is such, that he
" cannot turn and prepare himself by his
" own natural strength and good works to
" faith and calling upon God: wherefore
" we have no power to do good works plea-
" sant and acceptable to God, without the
" grace of God by Christ preventing us,
" that we may have a good will, and work-
" ing with us when we have that good will.
Here we are taught, that man by his fall is turned away from God, and has no strength to return, unless the grace of Christ go before to give him a good will, and then work with him when he has that good will. He has no strength in any of his faculties: they are all turned from God, and the grace of Christ alone is able to draw them back again. The understanding has no light. It is entirely in darkness, as to the things of God (*Eph.* iv. 18.) and the eye of the mind can no more enlighten itself, than the eye of the body can enlighten itself without light.

When

When the first ray of grace breaks in upon us, it finds us as it did the heathens at the coming of Christ sitting in darkness and in the shadow of death. And unless the rays of his grace shine into the understanding, it cannot be enlightened. Christ is the only light of the world. He is in the kingdom of grace, what the sun is in nature. Stop the influence of his bright beams, and the understanding will never see any reason to follow him, nor can the will choose him. The will of the natural man is depraved. It has a wrong bias, and is directly opposite to the will of God, and never can desire to be reconciled, unless the Holy Spirit draw it.

But does not the Holy Spirit's thus drawing it destroy our free-will? By no means: for it cannot destroy what is not. Fallen man has no free will but to sin; if that may be called free, " which is tied and bound " with the chains of sin," as our church expresses it. The scripture is absolutely positive upon this point, declaring (*Rom.* viii. 7.) " that the carnal mind (the will of our cor- " rupt nature) is enmity against God: for " it is not subject to the law of God, neither " indeed can be," until it be delivered from

the bondage and flavery of fin. It cannot be fubject to the will of God, unlefs his grace draw it to himfelf: for by nature it is drawn to fin. "The flesh always lufteth againft "the fpirit," fays the fcripture. "Fallen "man is of his own natur e inclined to evil," as our ninth article teaches. We run faft enough into evil. We want nothing to draw us. Sin ftrikes upon our nature and catches, like a fpark upon gun-powder. Surely we can all remember with what different tempers we ufed to go to the playhoufe, and to the church — how much greater delight we took in fpending an evening over the devil's books, at an innocent game at cards, as his children call it, than in reading the word of God. — And are there none of you, who now find more joy in many things, than you do in prayer? Thefe are evident proofs that you are ftill governed by the will of the flesh, which the fcripture fays lufteth always againft the fpirit, and therefore how can a defire ever arife in it after God or the things of God, unlefs Chrift draw it to himfelf? But the worft part of our corruption confifts in the depravity of our affections: for they are alfo governed by the will of the flesh, and are according to the apoftle to be crucified

cified (*Gal.* v. 24.) " And they that are " Chrift's have crucified the flefh with the " affections and lufts." And they that are not Chrift's are ftill under the power of the affections and lufts of the flefh. The heart, which is the commanding faculty, is in them fhut againft God, but is open to receive fin, loves it, dotes upon it, yea is fo enamoured of it as to prefer its fhort and empty joys to the folid felicity of an eternal heaven. And what power is able to break thefe chains? Who can fet our hearts at liberty, and turn them from fin to righteoufnefs? Who, but the fame God that created our hearts at firft. He alone can draw the affections from the love of the world, and from the love of fin and felf up to the things above, where Chrift fitteth at the right hand of God.

Upon all thefe accounts it appears, that man is incapable even of going to Chrift, and much more of running after him, unlefs he be drawn. The fcripture is exprefs, " No man can come unto Chrift, except the " Father draw him." Our church is clear in her opinion, " Such is the condition of " fallen man, that he cannot turn himfelf to " God, unlefs the grace of Chrift go before " to

" to give him a good will, and then work
" with him when he has that good will."
And this is also evident from matter of fact
and from experience. We find, that all
men by nature, instead of turning themselves
to Christ, who is the fountain of every good,
turn to sin which is the source of every evil.
Among learned and polite nations professing
christianity, there is the same ignorance of
the things of God, as among the darkest
heathens, the same depravity of the will, the
same corruption in the heart and the affections.
Which are clear and full proofs of our inability ever to go to Christ, unless he draw
us to himself. The speaker in the text saw
these proofs in a strong light. He found his
want of a Saviour, and he felt how unable
he was to do any thing towards attaining or
meriting the Saviour's love; he was quite
helpless, and without strength, therefore he
begs the grace of Christ would draw him.
My brethren, are you in this state? Do you
see the reasons, which I have now laid before you, in a clear and convincing light?
If not, may the ever-blessed God of whom
we are speaking draw you by his grace unto
himself; but if you are convinced, then you
will gladly follow me to the consideration

of

of the scripture method of drawing the soul to Christ, and this is the *second* point upon which I was to speak.

It is evident fallen man wants drawing to Christ, because the scripture has taught us the established method by which he draws us. The several steps of it are there particularly marked out for our instruction, that we might be certain how the work of grace advances in our own souls. The word of God is the outward means of drawing us. The Holy Spirit applying the word is the inward means. He begins his application by awakening the careless secure sinner, and by convincing him deeply and thoroughly of his being a sinful helpless creature. He shews him how entirely he is departed from God, and how unable he is to return, and then he makes him deeply sensible of his misery, until he does return. By which means the awakened sinner finds his want of a Saviour, and it is the daily prayer of his heart, that he may find pardon and peace through the blood of the Lamb of God; but at the same time he feels so much of his corruption, that he knows these prayers could never have arisen in his heart, unless the Holy Spirit had begun

begun to draw him unto Chrift. He who could before boaft of the light of nature, and of the great ftretch of his reafoning faculties, now finds nothing but blindnefs and darknefs in his underftanding. He who ufed to think highly of the dignity of humane nature, and of man's rectitude, and of the moral fenfe, &c. now fees that his will is by nature inclined to evil, and that our dignity and rectitude, and moral fenfe, are the mere chimeras of metaphyfical dreamers. Now he feels himfelf to be a poor loft finner, whofe heart and affections are fo far turned from God, that unlefs the Holy Spirit create in him a new heart he can never return. Being thus convinced of his finfulnefs and mifery, and of his own helpleffnefs to take one ftep towards his deliverance, he is prepared for the next work of grace, which is to draw him and to unite him to Chrift by faith. If the Holy Spirit had never convinced him of fin, he would never have found any want of a Saviour; and if he had never feen his own helpleffnefs, he would not have feen any neceffity for being drawn to Chrift by his grace; but being now convinced that he is both a finner and alfo a helplefs finner, the defires of his foul are drawn out after
God,

God, and he is in a right temper to wait upon God, until he be gracious unto him. And it is the office of the Holy Spirit to keep him waiting in the ways of the ordinances, until in God's due time he is sent to convince him of righteousness, and to bear witness with his spirit that the Father has accepted him and pardoned him through the merits of his beloved Son. Hereby he receives a well grounded faith in the obedience and sufferings of Jesus Christ. He can safely apply the merits of them to himself, and has great joy and peace in believing that they are imputed unto him for righteousness. He has the sure witness of this in himself, even the witness of the Holy Spirit, bearing testimony that Christ is his Saviour, and that God is his reconciled Father. This spirit of adoption enables him to cry Abba, Father, and to go to God with filial love and confidence. He now loves God because he knows that God first loved him, and thus he is drawn to God by the cords of a man, by the bands of love, and is ready through grace to give outward evidence of the reality of the inward work, by running after Christ in the way of his commandments.

Thus

Thus the Holy Spirit is the convincer of fin, and the convincer of righteoufnefs, and by thefe two convictions he draws the finner and unites him unto Chrift. He fhews him that he wants a Saviour, and then he fhews him his intereft in the Saviour. He firft makes him feel that he is a loft finner in himfelf, and then that he is faved by the righteoufnefs of Jefus Chrift. This is the eftablifhed method, in which the Holy Spirit draws the finner unto the Saviour, and this is a farther proof of its being neceffary he fhould be drawn, fince the fcripture has informed us both of the agent by whom, and alfo of the method by which, he is drawn unto Chrift.

My brethren, have you experienced this? Has the Holy Spirit drawn you from the love of fin and felf? Have you left the world, and all that is called great and happy in it to follow Chrift? Is no object more defireable than he is, in your eyes? Can you take up the crofs, and run after him with joy, although reproach, ridicule, and oppofition meet you at every ftep? Examine your own hearts, and try them by the certain effects, which follow upon the Holy Spirit's drawing

drawing the foul to Chrift; and this is the *third* particular in the text. Draw me, and " we will run after thee."

The natural man cannot follow Chrift, becaufe his heart and his affections are in another intereft. He loves to follow the world and its pleafures. And if he was convinced it was right to follow Chrift, he would meet with many infuperable difficulties, before he could fet out and run after him. But when the Holy Spirit draws him, he then removes that unwillingnefs which made the way appear fo difficult, and when he renews the faculties, he then gives them ftrength to overcome every difficulty. By his grace the inbred oppofition is fubdued. The underftanding is enlightened, and fees the way clearly; the will follows it readily; the heart and the affections purfue it chearfully. They follow their Lord and Saviour, whitherfoever he goeth. They run after him with eafe, in the way that was before difficult, with pleafure in the way, that was before painful, and with continuance in the way, wherein before they could not take a ftep. When the Holy Spirit has drawn the finner to Chrift, and really united him by faith

faith to the head of the myſtical body, he is then a new creature; old things are paſſed away, behold all things are become new, both in his ſtate and actions. The branch of the wild olive tree is grafted in and partakes of the root and fatneſs of the good olive tree, whereby its nature is changed. There is a real and an entire change made, which appears evidently to the common obſerver, by the outward change in a man's life and converſation. He acts upon different motives to what he did before. He purſues different ends and by different means. Before he run after the world, now he runs after Chriſt. Chriſt is now become all his treaſure, and the heart will be where its treaſure is, and where the heart is the other faculties will follow. No oppoſition ſhall diſcourage them. Let them be drawn and united to Chriſt, and none of his commandments will be grievous. Even ſelf-denial, the hardeſt commandment, will be eaſy. Place the love of Chriſt in the heart, and the man who before ſhrunk from and trembled at reproach, is nothing moved at it. He that was afraid of having his name caſt out with contempt, now can rejoice in being deſpiſed for Chriſt's ſake. He can give up

his

his character; he was once reckoned a learned and a good man, but now he can bear to be called a madman and a fool. He takes up his crofs daily, and runs on rejoicing. The contempt of the world haftens his fteps. It fpurs him on. It drives him nearer to his Saviour, and makes him live in clofer communion with him. If worldly men knew what infinite fervice they do us by their oppofition, they would alter their behaviour; for they are our real friends, though they do not intend us any kindnefs. They make us fit loofer and freer from the world than we otherwife fhould do, and when we are willing fometimes to take a little reft, and our love and zeal begin to abate fomething of their ardor, then they ftir us up, and make us mend our pace homewards. Thus the Holy Spirit caufes all things to work together for our good; even outward oppofition, fanctified by his grace, helps us forward, and enables us to run the fafter after Chrift: And I hope there are many of us, who can fay with the Apoftle, that nothing fhall feparate us from our blefled Lord and Saviour — " *I am perfuaded*, fays he, that neither
" tribulation nor diftrefs, perfecution, fa-
" mine, nakednefs, peril or fword, fhall be
" able

"able to separate us from the love of God, "which is in Christ Jesus our Lord."

My brethren, if you have been drawn to Christ, have these effects followed? Are you running after him in the ways of his commandments, and running with delight, as after the greatest happiness you can enjoy in time and in eternity? If this be your state, then in you is this scripture fulfilled. May he keep you by his almighty grace, and lead you on safely, until he draw you up to himself, and make you blessed with him for ever and ever. But if this be not your state, then it is incumbent upon me to warn you of your guilt, and of your danger, and to call upon you by every thing that is dear and valuable, to reflect seriously upon the situation you are in; and this brings me to the fourth and last particular upon which I was to speak. While I am applying it as closely as God shall enable me, Oh may he second my application by his grace, and carry it with his effectual working to every one of your consciences.

And first, in the spirit of love, I address myself to those persons, whose affections are
not

not drawn out after Chrift, by the fweet influence of his fpirit. Although Chrift has every beauty, every perfection in himfelf, and is willing to communicate to us of his fulnefs grace for grace, yet alas! few perfons defire him, and fewer run after him. You may eafily draw them to a play, to a concert, or to a ball; but to the God of all grace and glory what arguments, what motives can draw them? Propofe to them a fair opportunity of getting a great fortune, fhew them the way to honour and grandeur, their hearts meet the propofal with raptures: but change the difcourfe, and offer to them the ineftimable riches of Jefus Chrift, and the eternal honours and grandeur which he has to give, they feel no emotion. What can be the caufe of this ftrange inconfiftency? Whence is it, that men who love pleafure, fhould neverthelefs be fo abfurd, as to prefer fenfual to fpiritual, and temporal to eternal pleafures? nay fo monftroufly and wickedly abfurd, as to let the love of the world fhut out the love of that God who made it, and who will foon deftroy it. What can be the reafon of this? but that man is a corrupt fallen creature, depraved in every faculty of foul and body, infomuch that in fpiritual matters he is as

incapable

incapable of acting aright, as a dead man is of acting at all: for he is dead in trespasses and sins. Before he can move or stir a step he must be awakened, and convinced of his own helplessness. Then he will have reason to wait upon God for his help. But if he never finds himself sick, he will never send for the physician. If he be never convinced that he cannot go to Christ unless he be drawn, he will never desire the Holy Spirit to draw him. And if any of you be in this case, awake, thou that sleepest in death. Oh awake — awake — open thine eyes — and consider thy guilt. Whither can sin draw thee, but to hell? Consider thy danger, how near thou art to it. Thy heart and affections have never been drawn after Christ; but they are still placed upon those objects, which draw the love of all natural men unto themselves. Either money, or pleasure, or ambition are their favourite pursuits, so far as to exclude Jesus Christ, yea the very hungering or thirsting after him. You have not even a desire to experience his love. And therefore you may be assured, that you have no work of grace in you. You are still in your natural state. At an infinite distance from God. You have the

guilt

guilt of your nature and the guilt of your lives to anfwer for at his great tribunal. His holy law has already condemned you, and has paffed fentence upon you, threatening to pour out all its curfes upon your guilty heads. The righteous judge is bound to fee them executed upon you. And you know not how foon he may call you to judgment. Oh may God roufe up your fears, my brethren, and alarm you at the fight of your danger. Shall you, who fly with eager hafte from temporal danger, be eafy and carelefs, while the almighty God is your enemy, and he may this moment come and get glory to all his attributes by your everlafting deftruction? Can you think yourfelves fecure in this cafe, while there is only this little light vapour in your noftrils between you and hell? Lord Jefus forbid it. If any perfon hear me this day, who came hither without any intention to be made uneafy about the ftate of his foul, Oh let him now feel the mifery of being feparated from thee the fountain of good, and draw him to thyfelf, dear Lord, now draw his heart, from fin, and fatan, from the world, and the things of it, that he may follow me with profit, and be edified and comforted from what I have to apply,

Secondly, To those persons, whose desires the Holy Spirit has begun to draw unto Christ. I hope many of you are brought thus far, and can truly say, " Draw me, and we will " run after thee." If you can desire this sincerely, then the Holy Spirit has already begun to set your hearts at liberty. Wait upon him, and he will enable you to follow Christ with delight, whithersoever he calleth you. He will let you see so much of your want of Christ, and of his all-sufficiency to supply your wants, that you will resolve to give up all for him. You will see nothing more worthy of your pursuit, than the knowledge of your interest in Jesus. There is indeed nothing else worth your pursuit. Unless you are found in him, God the Father is your enemy, as you are a sinner in yourself; but when he sees you in the Son of his love, a living member of his body, all his blessings are yours in time and in eternity. Oh then be earnest, be unwearied at the throne of grace, until you are drawn effectually to Christ, and by faith united to him. Whatever keeps you from him, pray that it may be removed.
And

And be it ever so dear an object, a right hand or a right eye, look up to him, and he will give grace sufficient for you. If it be sin, he is almighty to save you from it. If it be great sin, his merits and righteousness are infinite. If they be many sins, what proportion do they bear to infinity? Are you a poor lost sinner, did not he come to seek and to save that which was lost? Are your sins of a deep die? The greatest have been pardoned. But none you think were ever so great as yours. How can that be? Is it not written, Jesus Christ came into the world to save sinners, of whom I, says *Paul*, am chief. But still the sense of your great unworthiness fills you with doubts and fears. You forget that Christ is the Saviour of the unworthy; and when he gives you *Paul's* faith, and you can say with him, Jesus Christ loved me, and gave himself for me, then your doubts and fears will fly before it. Whatever keeps you from closing in with Christ is an enemy to your soul. Pray therefore against it. Intreat the Holy Spirit to remove it, that you may be drawn to the loving Saviour of sinners, and united to him by living faith... And until he produce this grace in you, seek him diligently in all his ordinances. They are the instituted means by which he draws sinners to himself, and more closely unites believers. The word is the ordinance which he chiefly uses to the awakening of sinners. Glory be to him for that attractive virtue and powerful efficacy which still accompanies the preaching of it. By his blessing it is daily effectual to the convincing and converting of careless sinners, and to the building up, and establishing of believers. Wait then under it, and look up to God for the quickening Spirit to enable you to mix faith with what you hear. Be much in prayer. Pray to have your affections drawn from the world, and fixed upon God. Seek his presence in every ordinance, and when you find him in it, he will give you that grace which he intended it should convey. And thus persevere in the use of the means, until he bring you to the end. You shall find him whom your soul seeketh. He will draw you to himself, and then you will be able to run after him to whatever he calls you to do or to suffer. I hope there are several of you in this happy condition, and to you, my christian brethren, I address myself in the *third* and *last* place.

You

You know the truth of this scripture by your own experience. Having been convinced that you could not come unto Chrift, except the Father had drawn you by his good Spirit, you waited upon him, until he gave you faith, and united you to Jefus Chrift: Being united to the Lord and giver of grace and glory, all things are become yours. You are now the fons of God, and your heavenly Father will make all things work together for your good. You are heirs of God and joint heirs with Chrift: Oh remember then your privileges, and walk as children and fons of the moft high God. Keep near to your reconciled Father, and be ever looking to Jefus your dear Redeemer, and feek to be drawn nearer to him daily by waiting upon him in his ordinances, that you may have more of his life and love. And let the great things he hath done for your fouls be manifefted by your outward walking. Shew that you have nearnefs to God the Father through the Son of his love, and accefs with confidence through the faith that is in him. Let this appear by your living upon Chrift's fulnefs, and receiving from thence grace for grace. And the more grace you receive, in the ftrength of it run the fafter after Chrift for more grace. Run in the ways of his commandments. Follow his example. Prefs clofe after him in his fteps. And be affured the clofer you follow him upon earth, the nearer will you come to him in heaven. The more you are conformed to him in holinefs, the more fhall you be like him in glory.

Happy are you, my chriftian brethren, who have been thus drawn to Chrift, and are thus running after him. Hold on your courfe, determined in God's ftrength not to ftop upon account of what he fhall either call you to do or to fuffer. Purfue the way of duty, in which Chrift walked, whatever difficulties you may meet with, and fear not but he will give you ftrength to go on conquering and to conquer. Whatever his will is concerning you, rely upon him, and he will make you more than conquerors. You know where your ftrength is. God is your refuge and ftrength. Go to him in every hour of temptation, and he will give you grace fufficient for you. Afk and you fhall have. The Father will give whatever you afk in his Son's name. This is your great privilege, and God grant you may ever make ufe of of it in time of need. Let us now use it to crave a blessing upon what we have heard. And the whole of this discourse is excellently summed up in the collect of our church for this day.

" Grant to us, Lord, we beseech thee, the
" Spirit to think and do always such things
" as be rightful, that we who cannot do any
" thing that is good without the, may by
" thee be enabled to live according to thy will
" through Jesus Christ our Lord. *Amen.*"

SERMON III.

Chap. i. Ver. 4.

The upright love thee.

THE first part of this verse has been already considered. The person who speaks it, perceiving the form and comeliness of Christ, and finding a sweeter favour in his name than in the most fragrant ointment poured forth, was desirous of close union and spiritual fellowship with him. But being sensible of his own helplessness to come to Christ, had therefore prayed he might be drawn, " Draw me and we will " run after thee." The prayer was heard, and answered. Christ drew the soul by the cords of love unto himself, and as the following words shew, he brought it nigh, and gave it free access with confidence through the faith that is in him. He shed his love abroad in the heart, which drew it out in love to him. The believer found himself enriched with so many graces, and enjoyed such sweet communion with Christ, that he
rejoiced

rejoiced in him always, and declared that nothing but fin and ignorance could hinder men from feeing and admiring the excellencies of Jefus Chrift. If they were not in a fallen corrupt ftate, they would certainly admire and love him: for the upright love him.

If you were to afk the generality of men, who call themfelves chriftians, Whether they loved Chrift? They would anfwer, What do you think we don't love our Saviour? Moft certainly we do, for who can help loving him? We are taught to pray to him, and to love him from our very infancy, and we always have loved him.

But if you enquire upon what account they love Chrift? What knowledge they have of him and of his falvation, and what proof they can give of their love to him? They are then at a lofs. They can only tell you, that their parents had them baptized, and brought them up in the church of *England*, and that they keep conftant to their church, and have done their duty as well as they could, they never wronged any body, no one is without faults, and they have theirs.
This

This is the religion of the greatest part of our people, but how far short is this of the scripture character of one that loves Christ? A man may do all this, and much more, without one grain of love. He may practice many duties in his natural fallen state from several other motives than a sense of love to Christ, and a single eye to his glory. These are the christian motives to obedience, by which no natural man can be influenced. The Holy Spirit must have convinced him of his fallen state, must have raised him from it, must have opened his eyes to see what Jesus has done for his salvation, and must have shed abroad in his heart the love of God, before he can come up to the scripture character of them that love Christ: for they are upright who love him.

That we may have a clear and full view of the doctrine in the text, it will be proper to consider,

First, What is the scripture idea of the word *upright*.

Secondly, That man is not upright by nature.

Thirdly,

Thirdly, That he muſt be made upright before he can love Chriſt.

Fourthly, That being made upright he will ſhew his love to Chriſt by walking in love; and in the

Laſt place, I will draw ſome practical inferences from the whole. And may the Spirit of grace accompany and bleſs our meditations upon theſe particulars: may he direct our hearts into the love of Chriſt, and render what ſhall now be ſpoken upon it the means of increaſing it in all our ſouls. Under his guidance let us coſider

Firſt. What is the ſcripture idea of uprightneſs.

The *Hebrew* word which is here tranſlated *upright* is in the plural number. As a verb it is rendered to make ſtraight, *Iſaiah* xl. 3, 4. to direct in the way, *Iſaiah* xlv. 13. and to walk ſtraight in it, as 1 *Sam.* vi. 12. " And " the kine *took the ſtraight way* to the way " of *Bethſhemeſh*, and went along the high " way, lowing as they went, and turned not " aſide to the right hand or to the left."
This

This is its received sense in the lexicons; and from this idea the noun substantive is used for a directory, whatever guides in the right way, and the plural masculine denotes those persons who are in the right way, and who walk straight in it, whom we properly term upright men, alluding to their having been once in a fallen state, and having lost the right way, but being now raised up they are brought into it again, and made upright.

"Made upright," say our moralists, "how absurd is this expression! What necessity is there for making us upright? Are we not so by nature? Have not we all a moral rectitude? Have we not in ourselves the rule of right, and obligations to follow it? We are moral agents and upright, why then do you talk of making men what they already are?"

This is the language of modern reasoners, who would be wise above what is written. "For the soul that is lifted up, saith God, "is not upright in him." (*Hab.* ii. 4.) And yet the pride of their hearts loves flattering compliments, be they ever so false, and they are fond of being told of the dignity and rectitude of their nature, although these are

mere

mere metaphyfical chimeras. They are contrary to matter of fact, and to every day's experience, and contrary to the exprefs word of God, which proves that man is not upright by nature, as I am to fhew under my *fecond* head.

The whole volume of revelation gives us this character of mankind, " they have all " finned, and come fhort of the glory of " God." And what can be the dignity of a poor loft finner, who has robbed God of his glory? And where is the rectitude of fallen man, of whom " there is none righteous, no not one?" The fcripture ftrikes at the very root of our fancied dignity and rectitude, when it declares (*Mich.* vii. 2.) " There is " none upright among men," no not one is there in the rectitude of nature, in which man was at firft created: for " God hath " made man upright," faith another fcripture, " but they have fought out many in- " ventions," finful as well as foolifh, which prove that they are not upright as they firft came out of the hand of God. And indeed the fcripture fpeaks fo much of the fall and corruption of nature, as if it left man without any power or ftrength to recover himfelf.

The

The prophet *Jeremiah* praying to God says, (x. 23.) " O Lord I know that the way "of man is not in himself: it is not in man "that walketh to direct his steps." To which agree the words of the apostle (*Rom.* iii. 9, &c.) " We have before proved both "*Jews* and Gentiles, that they are all under "sin; as it is written, There is none righ- "teous, no not one, there is none that un- "derstandeth, there is none that seeketh "after God, they are all gone out of the "way:" so that there is no uprightness in any of them. Fallen man is gone out of the right way, and he does not understand how to return into it, nay he does not so much as seek after God, that he may be set right. His desires and his affections are turned from God: they are set upon sin, as our church expresses it in the ninth article, " Original sin is the fault and corruption of "the nature of every man ——— whereby "man is very far gone from original righ- "teousness, and is of his own nature inclined "to evil, so that the flesh lusteth always con- "trary to the spirit." How can man under the guilt of original sin have any moral recti- tude? Can he be upright who is very far gone from original righteousness? Can he

be

be in the right way who is very far gone out it? And how can he be inclined to love Chrift, who by the fault and corruption of his nature is always inclined to evil? While there is no fear of God before his eyes, how can there poffibly be any love of God in his heart. The love of Chrift is abfolutely inconfiftent with the blindnefs and depravity of fallen man, who is in love with fin. Sin and Chrift are as oppofite as heaven and hell, to which they lead. And as all fallen men are inclined to fin, and love it, the flefh lufting always contrary to the fpirit, confequently while they continue in this ftate, they cannot love Chrift; for none but the upright, who are raifed from their fallen ftate, love him.

Men and brethren, examine thefe authorities. Do they appear to you clear and decifive? Here are the exprefs words of fcripture, and the determination of our church upon this very point, declaring that man in his natural ftate is not upright. I would infer from your prefence here that you do believe this truth, and if you do, may it be a practical belief. Act under the fenfe of it. As you are convinced that you are not upright by nature, certainly you will feek to

be

be made upright, and will therefore gladly follow me to the *third* point I was to consider, *viz.* that you must be made upright before you can love Christ.

There is no other method, but what the gospel proposes. You would not go to the law, and set about keeping it more carefully for the future, in order to recover your rectitude: because the law allows of no failing. Upon the first offence it puts you under the curse, and condemns you. And as all have sinned and come short of the glory of God, therefore by the works of the law shall no flesh be justified in his sight. The law is a ministration of condemnation, it is useful to shew sinners that they are not upright, but it can afford them no hope, neither doth it offer them any remedy. It can only scourge and wound the conscience with the sense of transgression, and send the guilty to the gospel, for the recovery of their uprightness. And the gospel discovers to them the rich plan of grace, the covenant of the Eternal Three, with the distinct offices of each person in the œconomy of man's recovery. The Father's justice requires and receives, the Son's love pays, the Holy Spirit's grace applies,

plies, the atonement. The application is in the hand of the Spirit Jehovah. It is the work of his grace to apply to fallen man the benefits of the atonement, and to unite him by saving faith to Jesus Christ, whereby he is made upright.

The scripture has laid down, and all the upright have experienced, the method which the Holy Spirit pursues in bringing fallen man into a state of uprightness. First he shews the sinner his guilt and his danger, and lets him see that he is not upright. When the Holy Ghost the Comfortor is come, says our Lord, he will convince the world of sin. When he comes to the natural man, he finds him secure and unconcerned about the state of his soul or the pardon of his sins: for the whole world lieth asleep, yea dead in trespasses and sins, until awakened and quickened by the power of God's Spirit. He, that can be heard even by the dead, calls, " Awake, thou that " sleepest, and arise from the dead, and " Christ shall give thee life." This awakens and alarms the conscience. The sinner is made sensible of his guilt and condemnation, and convinced of his helplesness, and thus humbled

humbled under the fenfe of his want of uprightnefs, he is enabled to follow that divine teaching, which is to convince him where his wants may be fupplied.

He hears the report of the gofpel, that all finners who are fenfible of their wants may have them fupplied out of the exceeding riches of Chrift's grace, who has every thing to give that they can ftand in need of. They may receive out of his fulnefs grace for grace. Are they ignorant of the things of God? He is an all-wife prophet to enlighten their underftandings. Are they under the pollution and guilt of fin, and under the condemnation of the law? He is an all-meritorious prieft, whofe blood can cleanfe them from the pollution and guilt of fin, and by whofe righteoufnefs finners are freed from the condemnation of the broken law, and ftand accepted in the fight of the holy God. Are they enflaved and in bondage to their fpiritual enemies? He is an almighty king, who can fubdue in them the dominion of fin. When the awakened finner hears thefe things out of the gofpel, he affents to them as truths, and the Holy Spirit draws his defires out after the experience of them. As he is made to feel his wants, fo doth he wifh for a fupply from Chrift's fulnefs. He pants with fervent defire and earneft breathings of foul, to know his union with Jefus by faith, and would gladly receive him in all his offices? as a king to fubdue fin in him, as well as a prophet, and a prieft to free him from the guilt and deliver him from the punifhment of fin. The Holy Spirit cherifhes and ftrengthens thefe good defires, and in his own good time he compleats them, which is the third ftep in the work of experience.

He convinces the awakened finner of righteoufnefs, by giving him faith to believe that the righteoufnefs of Chrift is imputed unto him for juftification to life. The fcripture fays exprefsly, that it is his office to convince men of righteoufnefs, and thereby to give them peace in believing, that God the Father is reconciled unto them through the righteoufnefs of his Son: " For being juftified by " faith we have peace with God through " our Lord Jefus Chrift." (*Rom.* v. 1.) And when the mind is at peace with God upon account of its being juftified by faith, then it is made upright, and the evidence of juftifying faith is an upright walking. He that is in a juftified ftate is upright, and in confequence thereof he will in his life and
converfation

conversation walk uprightly. As he has received Christ Jesus the Lord, so he walks in him, and desires to live to the glory of his divine Saviour. He would have every thought, and word and work a testimony of his gratitude. It is the prayer of his heart, that he may walk worthy of the Lord unto all pleasing, and may shew forth the praises of his God by being fruitful in every good work: for " this is the love of God, that " we keep his commandments, and (to the " upright who keep them out of love) his " commandments are not grievous."

My beloved brethren, consider these things, and weigh them attentively. Have you been made to see the exceeding sinfulness of sin? That it has robbed you of your innocence and uprightness? That you are thereby exposed to the condemnation of the law, and to the wrath of infinite justice? Have you fled for refuge to Jesus? Do you perceive that he is the end of the law for righteousness unto you? And therefore knowing yourself upright in him, can you say, Christ is precious; he hath made me upright, therefore I love him; it is the grief of my soul to offend him; it is the greatest joy and delight

light of my heart to live and walk so as to please him? If you are as yet strangers to this happy knowledge, deceive yourselves no longer, do not think you have a sincere love to Christ: for you know not the power of Christ's love to you. But if you have been thoroughly humbled, and convinced of your lost helpless state, and have received Christ and his righteousness with love, joy, and peace, then being made upright, it is incumbent upon you to walk uprightly. It is your bounden duty to have a heart full of gratitude to God: and it is your privilege and happiness to be able to express your gratitude in your life and conversation. In them let it appear that you love Christ. Let the world see it in your christian walking, and give them continual occasion to glorify God on your account. And this brings me to the *fourth* particular I was to consider, namely, that being made upright, you will shew your love to Christ by walking in love.

When love is in the heart, it will appear outwardly. It will have its proper works. It will manifest itself, like light, and spread abroad its sweet influence. Light cannot propagate

propagate darkness, nor can the love of Christ produce hatred to his will: it is the doctrine of one apostle to his *Colossians*, chap. ii. 6. " As you have therefore received Christ " Jesus the Lord, so walk ye in him;" and of another apostle, " If any man saith, he " abideth in Christ, he ought himself also " to walk, even as Christ walked." (1 *John* ii. 6.) He is to prove that he abideth in Christ by following Christ's example, and by walking in his steps: for as Christ has made him upright, he will enable him to walk uprightly, because his outward walking is to bring glory to God, and good to to mankind. The love of Christ in the heart is that practical love which the apostle says is the fulfilling of the law: for it operates in the love of God and in the love of our neighbour, and on these two commandments hang all the law and the prophets.

The upright man has a lively sense of God the Father's being reconciled to him in Christ. Without this he could not love God: for a sinner, conscious of his having offended God and broken his holy law, can never be brought to love God until he be convinced that God loves him. He may as soon

soon love pain and torments, as love an offended God, whose almighty justice is to get itself glory by his destruction; but when he is persuaded that God is reconciled to him, then he has with joy and delight received the word of reconciliation: for "we "love him," not abstractedly, or metaphysically, but experimentally, " because he first " loved us." And when the Holy Spirit sheds abroad the love of God in our hearts, and reveals to them God's first loving us, then we see God in a new light. We look upon him as our reconciled Father, and in this character he appears altogether amiable and lovely. Having tasted how good and gracious he is, we desire from our hearts to please him, and this desire will certainly operate in the two great commandments, the love of God and the love of our neighbour.

The upright man loves God and walks with God. Love attracts, and unites, and thereby produces communion. The believer has communion with the Father and the Son by the bond of the Spirit; from whence are derived to him all the graces and blessings of the gospel, which he receives with a thankful heart, and shews his gratitude by

loving

loving what God loves. We know what God loves from his revealed will. This is the copy of his mind. And when the same mind is in us that was in Christ, then each of us shall be able to say, "I delight to do thy " will, O my God." The will of the upright man is reconciled to God's will, and therefore the way of the commandments becomes pleasant. There may be difficulties in it, but his love rejoices to overcome them. His spiritual enemies may tempt him out of the way, but love sets him above their temptations. When the world tries to share his heart with God, he rejects its offers with scorn, for he remembers that if any man love the world the love of the Father is not in him. Does it offer him pleasure? His love has found other kind of pleasure than the world has to give, even pleasures laid up at God's right hand for evermore. Does it offer him money? His affections are placed upon the unsearchable riches of Christ. There is his heart, and there is his treasure. Does it tempt him with honour? He desires only the honour that is of God. And thus love arms him against the temptations, which try to make his will act differently from God's will. His love being sincere he has upright intentions,

intentions, has a straight view of things, sees them with a single eye, and therefore is not easily drawn aside. God's glory is his one great end and aim. He has respect to it in every thing he does, and is as careful of avoiding whatever tends to injure it, as if it were wounding the apple of his own eye. And thus the upright man shews his love to God agreeably to what is written, " If " ye love me keep my commandments."

And his love to God not only enables him to do all things, but also to suffer all things. This is a very hard lesson to flesh and blood, but love makes it easy. Every disciple of Christ is called to follow him in the way of suffering. The cross is our portion. Self indeed would be gladly excused the taking it up, but love to Christ enables us to deny self, and to take up the cross daily : " For " love endureth all things." (1 *Cor.* xiii. 7.) Love can endure the sharpest cross, and christians have rejoiced and been exceeding glad in bearing it. They have had trials of cruel mockings and scourgings, yea moreover of bonds and imprisonment — They were stoned, they were sawn asunder, were tempted, were slain with the sword — They wandered

wandered about in deserts and mountains, in dens and caves of the earth, destitute, afflicted, tormented; and yet they were happy under all their sufferings. Many waters could not quench their love, nor could the floods drown it: for they loved not their lives unto the death. In the very flames they triumphed in their love to Christ, and in whatever shape death came they rejoiced in it, because it would bring them to their beloved Lord and Saviour Jesus Christ. And thank God we have still some men of the same spirit, who know in whom they have believed. Christ is dearer to them than life; and if he should call them to give proof of it, his strength would be perfected in them, and he would enable them to say with the apostle — " Who shall separate us from the
" love of Christ? Shall tribulation, or distress, or persecution, or famine, or nakedness, or peril, or sword? Nay in all these things we are more than conquerors through him that loved us: for I am persuaded, that neither death nor life, nor angels, nor principalities, nor powers, nor things present, nor things to come, nor height, nor depth, nor any other creature shall be able
" to

" to separate us from the love of God which
" is in Christ Jesus our Lord."

And after the upright man has thus learnt to do and to suffer all things out of love to Christ, he will certainly keep the second great commandment, which is like unto the first, and love his neighbour as himself. There is no brotherly love in the natural man. He may talk and write about it, but he cannot practice it sincerely and disinterestedly: because his views are narrow and selfish. St. *Paul's* character of the *Romans*, (chap. i.) is true of all natural men; they had every temper that was hateful, and they were haters of God and hating one another. But how then is brotherly love to be attained? It is from above, from whence cometh every good and perfect gift. The apostle *Paul* says, we must be taught it of God (*Thess.* iv. 9.) And another apostle says, " Let us
" love one another, for love is of God; and
" every one that loveth is born of God and
" knoweth God." From these scriptures it is evident, that God teaches us brotherly love, and when we are born of God, are made his adopted children in Christ, and know him to be our loving Father, then
have

have we that faith which worketh by love, to God and to man. This working love prays for, and labours to serve both their souls and bodies. It goes about doing them good, seeking opportunities, and willingly neglecting none. This is the upright man's walking with respect to his neighbour. He is knit to him in love, and shews it by the labour of love, by doing every kind and good office that is in his power. And thus he walks in love, as Christ hath loved him, which is the highest degree of brotherly love: for it is our Lord's new and great commandment, that we should " love one another as " he hath loved us."

Judge now, whether there be not good reason for the assertion in the text, " The " upright love thee?" Can sinners be sensible of Jesus's having done such great things for them, can they experience such a happy work wrought in them by the Divine Spirit and not love God? It is impossible. They have been made thoroughly sensible of their being by nature estranged from God, and wanderers from the right way, and of their having no power in themselves to return into it again. They found that they had no up-

rightness

rightnefs in them: for they loved what God hated; yea they hated God himfelf, becaufe he is the juft avenger of fin. But upon hearing the report of the gofpel, that Chrift will receive all finners who come unto him, they were ftirred up to come. And they waited upon Chrift, until the Holy Spirit brought them good tidings of great joy. He fhed abroad the love of God in their hearts, bearing teftimony with their fpirits, that God was their reconciled Father, and they were his adopted children in Chrift. And being thus made upright before God, in the ftrength of the Lord they walk uprightly. In their lives and converfations they make the two commandments, upon which hang all the law and the prophets, the rule of their actions, loving the Lord their God with all their hearts, and with all their fouls, and with all their ftrength, and their neighbour as themfelves. And thus they give evidence of their love to Chrift. This is the doctrine from which in the *fifth* and laft place I am to draw fome practical inferences.

And is what you have now heard agreeable, my brethren, to your experience? If it be, you are fafe and happy. If it be not,
I befeech

I beseech you suffer the word of exhortation. It is an awful and a solemn word, and may God accompany it with the effectual working of his power. If you were upright, you would love Christ, but as you do not love him, hear and tremble if you have any love left for your poor souls — " If any man " love not the Lord Jesus Christ, let him " be anathema maranatha." (1 *Cor.* xvi. 22.) Consider what it is to be under an anathema, to be cursed of God — cursed by his holy law; and to be finally excommunicated by that sentence which is never to be reversed — " Go ye cursed into everlasting fire." If you make light of this at present, yet unless you repent, a time will come when you will wish you had never been born, rather then have died under the anathema of God. Oh may he now touch the hearts of those ungrateful men who love not the Lord Jesus Christ, and may he of his grace and bounty give them to taste of that love, which passeth knowledge. May he that heareth prayer hear and answer, while I am speaking a word to the formalist, who has something of the shew, but no more of the power of divine love, than the careless sinner.

The formalift is rather decent in his outward behaviour — he attends regularly upon the ordinances — goes a great way in outward matters, and has the air and appearance of a chriftian. If you afk him, whether he loves Chrift, he is very confident he does, and is fomewhat offended that you fhould fufpect his love; but bring it to the teft of fcripture and it will not ftand the trial; for the formalift not only has not that true love of God, of which the fcripture treats, but he is alfo an enemy to it. He is the firft to cry out enthufiafm, if he hear, that the love of God arifes from the knowledge of our being reconciled to him in Chrift. It is with him the very mark of this new religious madnefs for any man to fay, that he loves God from a fenfe of his having freely forgiven him all trefpaffes. So that the formalift, with all his outward decency and profeffion, is rather farther from the true love of God than the carelefs finner: for the one has it not, but the other thinks it enthufiafm and madnefs to pretend to have it. And yet the fcripture is full of this enthufiafm. It has thus affigned the grounds and reafons of our love to God, " We love him, becaufe he " firft loved us."— Here we are taught, that
our

our love to him arises from his first loving us; but how can we know he first loves us, unless he manifest it, and shed it abroad in our hearts by the Holy Ghost. And in this way he does manifest it. He sends his good Spirit into our hearts to let us know that he first loves us. Hear ye formalists, the express testimony of God's word: " The " love of God is shed abroad in our hearts " by the Holy Ghost, which is given unto " us." (*Rom.* v. 5.) And until the Holy Ghost give you this love, be ye ever so decent in your outward walking, you have none of the life and power of religion, but are dead in your sins. This is the opinion of our church concerning you: for thus she teaches you to pray — O Lord, who hast taught us, that all our doings without charity (or love) are nothing worth: send thy Holy Ghost and pour into our hearts, that most excellent gift of charity (or love) the very bond of peace and of all virtues, without which whosoever liveth is counted dead before thee, &c. (*Collect for Quinquagesima.*) Charity signifies nothing more than love. And in this collect the sense, as well as the epistle to which it refers, determine it to be the love of God; and if you have not this love

love poured into your heart by the Holy Ghoſt, let whatever elſe be in your heart, you are counted dead before God. Oh that he may bring you out of that dead lifeleſs ſtate, in which you are at preſent, and raiſe you up to newneſs of life, and place you among the upright who love Chriſt. And

Whatever others may do, the upright will love Chriſt. Though other men may ſee no form nor comelineſs in him that they ſhould deſire him, yet in their eyes he is altogether lovely. They love him for making them upright, and they give evidence of their love by walking uprightly. His will is theirs. They love what he loves. His revealed will is the copy of his mind, and therefore it is the rule of their converſations. Being made upright, and the ſame mind being in them that was in Chriſt, there will be the ſame outward walking. They will follow his example, and tread in his ſteps: for how can their love to Chriſt act againſt its own nature, ſo as to hate his will? Certainly therefore their love to him will ſhew itſelf in love to his commandments. And if a man ſay, I love Chriſt, and hateth his commandments, he is a liar, for he that loveth not the will

of

of God, how can he love God? And this commandment have we from him, that he who loveth God loveth his commandments also.

Is this your experience, my brethren? Enquire strictly, and intreat the Holy Spirit to help you in enquiring, whether Christ has made you upright, and you therefore love him and his commandments. I have put you upon this enquiry, because the scripture puts you upon it, and because there is a general mistake concerning it. The scripture has expressly mentioned the effects, which will flow from the love of Christ in the heart; these effects we desire you to manifest in your lives. We don't send convinced sinners to the law, and tell them, If ye would enter into life, keep the commandments. No. We send them to Christ, because they have broken the commandments, and they must be pardoned, and receive justification to life from him, before they can keep any one commandment well-pleasing to God. But when the Holy Spirit gives them the knowledge of their pardon and justification, then they receive a faith that worketh by love, a faith that proves itself to be from God by working in love to what God loves. These workings of faith by love to God and man are the marks and evidences we desire to see in your lives and conversations. We are authorised from God's word to call upon you for them, not as if they were your salvation, but as the certain effects of your being in a state of salvation. The sun cannot be without sending out light: so love cannot be without producing its proper works — works as certainly flowing from it, as light does from the sun. If works flow not out, we are certain there is no love in the heart: for there is no cause, if there be no effects. Examine then, I beseech you, the nature of the love which you think you have to Christ; see if it has the scripture marks of true love. Happy is he who looking into his own breast is able to say, " Lord, thou knowest all things, thou " knowest that I love thee: whom have I " in heaven but thee, and there is none up- " on earth I desire in comparison of thee." My brethren, can you take up these words, and repeat them with praise and thankfulness? If you can, may you go on rejoicing, daily receiving larger measures of divine love, and bringing forth richer and riper fruits to

the

the glory of God. But if you cannot, do you see your want of love to Chriſt, and are you hungering and thirſting after it? If you are, look up and aſk it of the God of love. Pray him to beſtow it upon you out of the riches of his free grace. And let us all with one heart and one voice intreat him in the words of our church to give us the experience of what has been now ſaid, praying as ſhe hath taught us. — " O almighty
" God, who alone canſt order the unruly
" wills and affections of ſinful men: grant
" unto thy people, that they may love the
" thing which thou commandeſt, and de-
" ſire that which thou doſt promiſe, that ſo
" among the ſundry and manifold changes
" of the world, our hearts may ſurely there
" be fixed where true joys are to be found;
" through Jeſus Chriſt our Lord. *Amen.*"

SERMON IV.

Chap. i. Ver. 7.

Tell me, O thou whom my soul loveth, where thou feedeſt, where thou makeſt thy flock to reſt at noon.

THESE words are part of a prayer, which the faithful offer up to the great and good ſhepherd. He had drawn them to himſelf, had pardoned all their wanderings, and had ſhed his love abroad in their hearts, which made them pray for his ſupport and defence. They ſtill found that they had many wants, for which they expected a ſupply out of his fulneſs, and many infirmities, from which they deſired deliverance in his ſtrength. His grace was needful every moment. That ſpiritual and divine life, which he had begun in their ſouls, could not be carried on without his continual help. They wanted the bread that cometh down from heaven, and which is the life of the ſpirits of men,

as

as much as they want the bread which is the life of the body. And in time of trouble they wanted divine strength. When assaulted with powerful temptations from within and from without, they durst not think of attacking them, and much less of overcoming them with the arm of flesh, but they sought to be strong in the Lord and in the power of his might. This is the subject of the words now read; in which the faithful pray the great and good shepherd to tell them where he feeds his flock, and where he shelters them from the scorching heat of the sun at noon — " Tell me, O thou whom my " soul loveth, where thou feedest, where " thou makest thy flock to rest at noon." Here we have

First, The amiableness of Christ's pastoral office; every faithful soul can say to the good shepherd, " O thou whom my soul loveth."

Secondly, The reason assigned for loving him, he feedeth his flock like a shepherd. And

Thirdly, He gives them comfort and strength in the time of great trials, he makes

his

his flock to reſt in the burning heat at noon. And

Fourthly, He ſaves his flock from the great trial of all, from death.

And while I am ſpeaking to theſe particulars, may the Spirit of the living God apply them to all your hearts. May he convince you practically of the amiableneſs of Chriſt's paſtoral office, that you may be able to ſay from your own experience, " O thou " whom my ſoul loveth." Chriſt is the good ſhepherd, and in this character he is altogether lovely. It is one of the ſweeteſt relations that he ſtands in to his people, and is to them the fulleſt of comfort; but then they muſt derive their comfort from knowing him to be their ſhepherd, and themſelves to be his people and the ſheep of his paſture. Without this knowledge, ſpeaking of his lovelineſs would be like talking in an uknown tongue: for what excellency can ſinners ſee in him that they ſhould deſire him, if they were never convinced that they were loſt ſheep, who muſt for ever periſh, unleſs the good ſhepherd bring them back again into his fold? They ſee no form or comelineſs in
him,

him, until they begin to find their want of him, and therefore when grace comes, its firſt work is to convince them of their wants. The firſt ſtep it ſets them in their way to God is to make them ſenſible of their having wandered from him. And all of you, my brethren, whatever your ſtate may be at preſent, had wandered from God. You had gone every man after the error of his own ways, and in the maze of theſe errors you had wandered ſo long that you were quite loſt. You could not diſcover the way back again to God, or if any one was to ſhew it you, you had neither will nor power to take one ſtep in it. Sin had impaired, yea had deadened the faculties of the ſoul. It left the underſtanding in darkneſs, the will corrupt and always inclined to evil, and the heart and affections at enmity with God. In this loſt and helpleſs ſtate, and this is the ſtate of every man by nature, you were like ſheep that have wandered from the fold. This is a common image in ſcripture. Fallen man is there compared to a loſt ſheep, and this is a juſt and beautiful picture of him: for ſheep, as you all know, are ſimple weak creatures, who have neither force to reſiſt their enemies, nor wiſdom to avoid them;

they

they want sagacity to find out the best pastures, to defend themselves from the inclemency of the weather, and to find the way back again to the fold after they have once strayed from it. There is not a creature in the world more helpless than a lost sheep. It must perish unless the shepherd seek it out and bring it back. Now all the sons of *Adam* are in this lost and helpless condition, and the first step towards their deliverance is a conviction of their not being able to do any thing towards delivering themselves. Whether they be learned or unlearned, rich or poor, they are alike wanderers from God, and alike unable in their own strength to return. It is exceeding difficult to convince natural men of this truth, and yet the gospel can do them no good, until they be convinced. They must see, that they are poor lost sheep before they will seek after the salvation which the great shepherd has purchased for them; and because it was necessary they should see themselves in this state, God has therefore been pleased to give them abundant proof of their being in it. The prophet *David* says (*Psalm* cxix. 176.) " I have gone astray, like a lost " sheep, seek thy servant." But lest this should be thought his own particular case,
God

God by the mouth of another prophet declares that it is the cafe of us all. "All we like sheep have gone astray, we have turned every one to his own way." (*Isaiah* liii. 6.) Here all men without exception are said to have gone astray like sheep, and to have turned from the way of God to their own ways, and naturally they are like lost sheep, helpless and unable to return. The people of the *Jews* were certainly in this condition: for our Lord says, he was sent to the lost sheep of the house of *Israel*, and not to them only, as if they alone were lost: for "other sheep, says he, I have, which are not of this fold, them also I must bring" (back again to God from their wanderings, therefore they were lost sheep as well as the *Jews*) "and there shall be one fold and one shepherd."

If the sense of these scriptures was not clear, and their authority decisive, I might bring more proofs, but I hope these are sufficient. They must be satisfactory to the members of our church, because this is her established doctrine both in her articles and homilies. The homilies upon the misery of man are written entirely upon this subject, and

and the tenth article says, that such is the condition of man after the fall, that he cannot turn or prepare himself to any good, unless the grace of Christ go before to give him a good will, and then work with him, when he has that good will. If you never found yourself unable to do any good unless Christ should give you both the will and the power, you may call yourself a member of our church, but you are indeed a stranger to her constitution. And though you attend upon her ordinances, and take her words in your mouth, yet you deny them in your heart. What a mockery is it of God for a man to come to church, and upon his bended knees in the presence of an all-seeing God to declare (which you have all done this day) " Almighty and most merciful father, we " have erred and strayed from thy ways like " lost sheep," and afterwards to confess " There is no health in us." Is not this mocking God to his face, if a man does not believe, or does not experience what he says? Let every person, who would be thought a member of our church, weigh the force of these words, and if he cannot subscribe to his being a wanderer from God, and as unable to return as a lost sheep, never more let

him

him join with us in our church's confeſſion, until he can ſay from his heart, that he has erred and ſtrayed from God's ways, like a loſt ſheep, and has no health in himſelf, or ſtrength to return.

It is then a plain matter of fact, that fallen man is in a loſt helpleſs condition. He is in it, but the worſt part of his fall conſiſts in his being inſenſible of his danger. He is loſt, but he does not know it; he is helpleſs, but his pride gives him high ideas of his own ſtrength. While he continues in this ſinful ſecurity, he ſees no want of a ſhepherd; and though he never ſends up one wiſh or prayer for help, yet the great and good ſhepherd does not forget his own. He is Jehovah, the true ſelf-exiſting God, the creator of all things viſible and inviſible; and this almighty and eternal Being vouchſafes to reveal himſelf to his people under the ſweet and amiable character of a ſhepherd. Whatever is lovely in an earthly ſhepherd is to be found ſpiritually in our incarnate God. Is it expected of a ſhepherd, that if he loſe any of his flock he ſhould ſeek diligently until he find it? Is he to ſpare no pains, to refuſe no difficulty or danger in ſearch of it? Herein we have a beautiful

beautiful image of our Lord's paſtoral love. He looked down from heaven upon the children of men, and ſaw them wandering every one after the error of their own ways, he ſaw that deſtruction and miſery were in their ways, he ſaw the enemy of their ſouls, like a roaring lion, going about and ſeeking whom he might devour. His eye pitied them. At the ſight of their loſt and helpleſs condition the bowels of his tendereſt compaſſion were moved. He could not ſee them periſh; and therefore he came down from his eternal throne, veiled the brightneſs of divine glory under a tabernacle of fleſh, humbled himſelf to the loweſt abaſement, to be born a ſervant under the law, to ſuffer, to die, yea the accurſed death of the croſs. To this infinite condeſcenſion he ſtooped in order to ſave his loſt ſheep. This he expreſsly declares was the gracious purpoſe for which he came into the world: " The Son of Man is come " to ſeek and to ſave that which was loſt." Even they whom he has ſought and ſaved were loſt as well as others, and as helpleſs as loſt ſheep. They had no deſire, and much leſs power to return to God, but were pleaſing themſelves with the errors of their own ways, when the Lord Jeſus ſtopt them.

He

He called to them, and gave them ears to hear. He spake, and gave them hearts to obey. He drew them to himself, and saved them with a great salvation. And thus he was found of them that sought him not. And whoever thou art, whom he has sought, thou hast been made to see thy wanderings. If thou art indeed brought home to God, thou hast been deeply humbled for thy turning away from him; and thou art convinced that if Jesus Christ had not come down from heaven to seek thee, thou must have been lost for ever and ever. But now, being sought out by his tender care, and found, thou canst tell of the love of this good shepherd, who has not only brought thee home to God, but has also pardoned thee, washed thee clean in his own blood, and justified thee with his infinite righteousness. Thou art now admitted into his fold, and the sense of what he has already done for thee will enable thee to go to him continually with faith, and say, " Tell me, O thou whom " my soul loveth, where thou feedest; from " what I have already experienced of thy " love, I doubt not but thou wilt feed me " with the bread that endureth unto ever-" lasting life." And this leads me *secondly* to confider a reafon here affigned for loving him, namely, that he feedeth his flock like a fhepherd.

The earthly fhepherd is not only to bring back the loft fheep, but it is alfo part of his paftoral office, to provide for its future fupport. He is to fee that it lack nothing, but is to feed it in green paftures, and to lead it befide the ftill waters. And herein we have a lively picture of our Lord's paftoral love. When mankind left God and turned into the ways of fin, they loft that divine fupport, which is the happinefs of the foul, and they were feparated from the fountain of life. The apoftle fays, they were alienated from the life of God. And they had no means to recover it, nor indeed any fenfe of their want of it. They were laying dead in trefpaffes and fins, when the Lord Jefus brought it down for us from heaven, and they are ftill in this dead ftate, when he fends his good Spirit firft to convince them how much they want it, and then freely to beftow it upon them: " For the bread of God (that " bread which fupports the life of God in " the foul) is he, which cometh down from " heaven, and giveth life unto the world."

This

This is our Lord's account of himself. He came down from heaven to give this bread of God unto a world dead in sin, and whenever a sinner receives it of him, then he begins to live unto God. This bread is the support received from Christ's body and blood, from the merits of his obedience and sufferings, which are applyed to the sinner by the Holy Spirit, and made effectual by the reviving streams of his grace. And this method of feeding his flock is beautifully painted in the 23d *Psalm*; the truth of which every believer experiences as well as *David*, and can therefore truly say, " The Lord is
" my shepherd, therefore can I lack no-
" thing: he shall feed me in green pastures,
" and shall lead me forth beside the waters
" of comfort. He shall convert my soul,
" and lead me in the paths of righteousness
" for his name's sake." The sheep of the Lord's pasture lack nothing: for he supports them with all things that pertain to life and godliness; and when they find themselves thus supported, they will be full of love to their good shepherd, and they will love the means, which he has appointed to convey nourishment to his flock. In these means they have grown in grace, their love has
increased,

increased, and their hearts have been more inflamed with pure affection to their divine shepherd, and therefore they can always join with the believers in the text in desiring to be led by his grace, to the places and means, in which he feeds his flock. " Tell me, O "thou whom my soul loveth, where thou "feedest thy people, and the sheep of thy "pasture."

My brethren, can you join with them? Is the good shepherd altogether lovely in your eyes for giving you the bread of God which cometh down from heaven? Have you received it from him? Do you find it strengthening your hearts, enabling you to die more to sin, and to live more to God, to get power over inward corruption, and outward opposition. Happy are ye, if this be your case, for you need not fear his comfort and strength in time of great trials and troubles, as it follows in the *third* part of my text, he will make his flock to rest in the burning heat at noon.

The heat of the sun at noon is in *Judæa* very violent and scorching. The faithful shepherd will take care to drive his flock during

during thefe fultry hours to fome cool fhade. There he will defend them from their enemies: for they are weak and defencelefs themfelves. All the beafts of prey can with eafe devour them, and in hot countries where the beafts of prey abound, the fhepherd is forced to watch his flock in the cold of the night, as well as in the heat of the day: for thus we find *Jacob* defcribing his care of *Laban's* flock, " I was in the day confumed " with heat, and with froft in the night, " and my fleep departed from mine eyes." And in the *New Teftament* we read, that in the depth of winter, when our Lord was born, there were fhepherds in the open field watching over their flocks by night. How beautifully is our Lord's paftoral care hereby reprefented? For the fhepherd of *Ifrael* never flumbers nor fleeps, watching over his flock continually night and day, and he fuffers no enemy to come near to hurt them. He himfelf is a fhadow in the day-time from the heat, and a fafe refuge from the power of all their enemies. They have a formidable hoft to contend with. Sin, and fatan, and the world, and the temptations and troubles in it, had taken captive the loft fheep, and law and juftice allowed them to be kept in bondage,

bondage, until death should seize upon them, and deliver them over to the place of torments, where the worm dieth not, and the fire is not quenched. From these enemies the Lord Jesus came to save his flock. He subdued all these enemies in his own person, and does subdue them by the grace of his almighty Spirit in all his people. When he has fought them, and brought them back to God, and fed them with the bread of life, then in the strength of this bread he enables them to fight against their enemies, who are also his, and it is for his glory that they get the victory over them. The weaker they are, the more does his strength appear, which worketh mightily in them and by them. And to encourage them to fear nothing but sin, he thus exhorts them — " Fear not little flock, for it is your " Father's good pleasure to give you the " kingdom;" and as it is his good pleasure to give you the kingdom itself, he will certainly support you in the way to it. You may be poor and weak sheep, but your shepherd is the Lord God omnipotent. You may have many infirmities, but he knows them, and is touched with the feeling of them. You may have many temptations,

but

but he will not suffer you to be tempted above what he will enable you to bear. Your troubles may be great, but he says, " Fear not, for I am with thee, I will be with thee in trouble, yea, I will deliver thee, and bring thee to honour." Who can doubt of his pastoral love, that reads this sweet description of it in *Isaiah*, " He shall feed his flock like a shepherd, he shall gather the lambs with his arm, and carry them in his bosom, and shall gently lead those that are with young." In what a tender and affecting manner is our Lord's pastoral love here represented? He feeds all his flock, so that they lack nothing. If any of them wander from the fold, he gathers them with his arm. Those that are with young he leads gently. And those that cannot go at all, he carries in his bosom, and lays near his heart. Oh what a wonderful love is this! Certainly there never was greater love, except what our Lord shewed, when he laid down his life for the sheep. In which instance of his love he is unrivalled. Other shepherds may have such care for their flock, as to seek the lost sheep, to feed them all, to watch over them, and to defend them from their enemies, and nothing farther is expected of them. But our Lord shewed his greatest love, where theirs ends. They feed and fatten the flock, that they may feed and cloath themselves with it. They live upon the flock; but he laid down his life for the helpless lost sheep. He died to give them life: for the good shepherd giveth his life for the sheep; which leads me to the *fourth* particular I was to consider, namely, That Christ saves his flock from the great trial of all, from death.

The faithful in the text certainly included this, when they prayed for a resting-place from trials and troubles. The raging heat at noon properly expresses the sharpest trial with the last enemy. When sin and satan try their utmost efforts, and set the King of terrors to attack and alarm the conscience. And they succeed with all natural men. To unpardoned sinners how fearful is death. The approach of it is to them the beginning of endless sorrows. But our Lord's pastoral love has engaged to deliver the sheep of his pasture from the power and from the fear of death. And here his divine affection for them shines forth in a wonderful manner, which can no more be described, than it
can

can be imitated: for if all the holy angels in heaven, and all the creatures in the universe were to lay down their lives to save one lost sheep, it would be in vain. The Lord Jesus alone was equal to this great work: for he was God and man united in one Christ, and therefore his death was of inestimable and infinite value. By it he made a full, perfect, and sufficient sacrifice, oblation, and satisfaction for sin. St. *Paul* tells the *Corinthians*, " I delivered unto you first " of all that which I also received, how that " Christ died for our sins according to the " scriptures." The scriptures of the *Old Testament* shewed in the sacrifices of the law, that he was to die and to shed his blood for sin. One prophet says, that Christ should swallow up death in victory. (*Isaiah* xxv. 8.) And in another Christ himself says, " I " will ransom them from the power of " the grave, I will redeem them from " death: O death, I will be thy plagues, " O grave, I will be thy destruction." (*Hosea* xiii. 14.) And the *New Testament* shews how he fulfilled these scriptures; by the one sacrifice of himself he abolished death, so that it has no longer any power over the children of God.

But

But do not the children of God die as well as other men? Yes. It is appointed unto all men once to die; but death has no power to hurt God's children, and they know, by faith, that it has not. Here is their comfort. Each of them can say with *Paul*, Jesus Christ loved me and gave himself for me. By his death I live. I know him, and the power of his resurrection: for I have experienced this power raising me up from the grave of sin to newness of life, and therefore when I go through the shadow of death I will fear no evil, for thou my almighty shepherd shalt be there with me, and thy rod and thy staff shall then comfort me.

And thus Christ has delivered the sheep of his pasture from the power of death, and thanks be to God who gives us the victory over the fear of it through Jesus Christ our Lord. He came to deliver those, who through fear of death had been all their lifetime subject to bondage. And he does deliver them. We see many happy instances of his power to deliver. And if there be any of you, my brethren, whose hearts tell you that you are not delivered, consider what

is the reaſon. Why do you, who call yourſelves chriſtians, fear to die? What is there
terrible in death to a true believer? And yet
it is terrible to you; if it ſhould come this
day, it would ſurpriſe you. Nay the very
thought of it is painful. You put it aſide,
and wiſh to forget it. All this proves that
you have nothing more of chriſtianity than
the name. You have experienced none of
the life and power of it: for your ſins are
not pardoned. You fear death, becauſe the
ſenſe of guilt is not taken out of the conſcience. " For the ſting of death is ſin,
" and the ſtrength of ſin is the law." While
ſin ſtings the conſcience, and the broken law
gives ſtrength to ſin, ſo that it ſtings the
deeper, you muſt fear death. And this is
the reaſon ſo many people called chriſtians
are afraid to die. They don't know that
their ſins are pardoned, and that all the
demands of the law upon them are ſatisfied,
by their good ſhepherd's laying down his
life for them. Nay they are ſo far from
knowing this, that they never deſired, and
perhaps many of them think it preſumption
and madneſs to pretend to know it. My
brethren, if theſe be your thoughts, you
may be aſſured, you can never meet death
with

with joy, until faith give you a clear view of your interest in Christ: but when it enables you to see him, obeying, suffering, and dying for your sins, and as your all-prevailing intercessor pleading your cause before God, then the sting of death will be taken away. You will have nothing to fear: for then you will know, that all things are yours, whether life or death, or things present or things to come, all are yours, and ye are Christ's, and Christ is God's.

If we sum up, and lay together what has been said, it will appear that Christ is altogether lovely in the character of the shepherd and bishop of our souls. What more could be done, than he has done for the sheep of his pasture? He has brought them back to God from the error of their ways, has supported them when they were brought back, has defended them in their trials and troubles, and has given to them eternal life as the purchase of his death. These with all the other benefits of the gospel were obtained by the good shepherd's laying down his life for the sheep, and are now freely bestowed by his grace, and thankfully received by faith. At present it is the great privilege

privilege of all Chrift's fheep to know by faith that they belong to his fold, and that they have an intereft in the bleffings which he has to give. Thefe faith receives and enjoys: for we are in poffeffion of none of them, until they be applied, and it is faith that makes the application. When we receive faith from the operation of God, then we know that all the benefits which the good fhepherd has to beftow are ours: for the language of faith is this — " The Lord is *my* " fhepherd, therefore can I lack nothing. " He fhall feed *me* in a green pafture, and " fhall lead *me* forth befide the waters of " comfort. Yea though I walk through the " valley of the fhadow of death, I will fear " no evil." When faith fears no evil, no not even death, than hope can reft itfelf upon the care of the good fhepherd, and the fenfe of his love will produce love and grateful obedience. Thus the graces of the Spirit, faith, hope and love, are produced in the hearts of all that belong to Chrift's flock, and are the fheep of his pafture. They know their good fhepherd, and are known of him. They know his voice and follow him, yea they follow him with joy, whether

he

he calls them to do or to suffer for his name's sake.

If any of you think this is not to be clearly known, your denial does not prove, that God has not promised to give this faith, nor that he does not give it, but only that he has not given it to you; for the scripture has expresly promised it, and it is a certain matter of fact, that God is daily fulfilling his promises. And when they are fulfilled to any person, he cannot but know it. He had been all his life a lost sheep, wandering from God without any desire to return, does not he know, when he began to pray earnestly, that God would heal his wanderings, and bring him home again? How can he possibly be ignorant of so great a change in his own mind? When his desires take a new turn, he that sought for happiness in the world, now seeks it in Christ, and has turned his back upon all that worldly men call rich and honourable, desiring only the riches of grace, and the honours of eternity, how can the man himself not know this, when every body about him sees it? When God has given him these desires, and he is resolved by the help of divine grace to seek
until

until he find by faith, that Chrift is his Saviour and his God, when his conftant difcourfe is, " Nothing but Chrift, nothing but " Chrift," does not the man know all this time what he is fpeaking and doing? Its certain he does, becaufe his neighbours know it and ridicule him for it, and when they cannot laugh him out of his religious notions, they leave him for an incorrigible enthufiaft. But if he does not leave feeking God, God will convince him by many undoubted proofs, that he is one of the fheep of Chrift's pafture. God will enable him to know that he is a partaker of all the exceeding great and precious promifes of the gofpel by means of his union with Jefus Chrift through faith, and he will fend the fpirit of adoption into his heart, bearing teftimony with his fpirit, that he is a child of God. This teftimony cannot poffibly be a delufion, becaufe it is followed by a change, which the Almighty alone is able to effect: for being united to Jefus by faith, he is made partaker of a new nature, with a new heart, and renewed affections; he is a new creature, the old things of his former ftate and converfation are done away, and behold all things are become new. His foul is filled with love

love to his God and Saviour, for doing thefe great things for him, and fhew its love by love to his commandments. When all this is done, may not the man confidently fay with the prophet, " The Lord is *my* fhep-
" herd, I am one of his people, and one
" of the fheep of his pafture."

Since then believers may be as certain of Chrift's being their fhepherd, as they were in the text, and can truly fay with them, " Tell me, O thou whom my foul loveth, " where thou feedeft thy flock, where thou " makeft them to reft in the raging heat of " noon," I have now brought the difcourfe to the point I aimed at, which was to prepare the way for this queftion, and may God enable you to anfwer it to yourfelves honeftly and fairly, " Is Chrift *your* fhepherd? Let every one of you afk his own heart, " Is " my foul under the paftoral care of this " good fhepherd?" If you know by the marks before laid down, that he is yours, and you are the fheep of his pafture, you will love him and ferve him without fear in holinefs and righteoufnefs before him all the days of your life. But if you know it not, or are not feeking it, it is incumbent upon

me

me to warn you of your guilt, and of your danger. You know not as yet that you have any right to use the words of the text. You cannot say to the great and good shepherd from a sense of what he has done for you, " O thou whom my soul loveth." You know not that he feeds you with the bread of God, which endureth unto everlasting life, nor that he is your defender in danger, your refuge in time of trouble, your ready helper in an hour of temptation, and your almighty supporter under persecution. Nay perhaps you may think these things cannot be known. From hence it is certain, that you are not at present a part of Christ's flock, and therefore you have none of the blessings or privileges which belong to it, no pardon of sin, no sense of justification to life, you have none of the life which Christ came to give to sinners, no grace, no holiness, no happiness. God the Father is your enemy, his law has condemned you, his justice is concerned to see the sentence of the law executed upon you, and the judge himself has given you an awful description of its execution in the xxvth of St. *Matthew*. Consider these things, my brethren. Weigh the importance of them, and see whether you

I have

have not reason to look up to the great and good shepherd, and to intreat him to bring you back to God from the error of your ways. May the Spirit of the living God shew you the danger of your present state, and stir up desires in your hearts for deliverance. May he enable you to seek it as his free gift, and in the ways of his ordinances, until you experience the sweet and comfortable doctrine in the text, and can join in gratitude and praise with the Lord's people, and the sheep of his pasture, to whom I shall in the last place make a short application.

My christian brethren, you have experienced the love of the divine shepherd, and therefore you love him, and can with full trust and confidence address him in the words of the text, " O thou, whom my " soul loveth." In the sense of this love you are happy. Knowing that the incarnate God stands related to you as your all-loving shepherd, you can cast all your care upon him: for he careth for you. He has engaged, and your faith can rest itself upon his promises, that you shall lack nothing. All things are yours: for they are in the
hand

hand of your kind shepherd and loving Saviour, who will make them all work together for your good. He knows what is best for you, and he will give it you. And you know it to be best; be it sickness or health, poverty or riches, they are alike sanctified visitations. You taste of God's love in them, and you love him for them. Nothing can hurt you but sin, and you need fear nothing but it: for all things but sin shall do you good. Outward trials and troubles shall be real blessings. They will drive you nearer to Christ, and keep you in closer communion with him, and thereby you will not only be a conqueror over them, but will also make great advances in the divine life. " What shall separate us from
" the love of Christ, says the apostle. Shall
" tribulation, or distress, or persecution, or
" famine, or nakedness, or peril, or sword?
" Nay, in all these things we are more
" than conquerors through him that loved
" us."

Now is not this a state greatly to be desired? If something did not blind men's eyes and pervert their judgment, would not they all out of self-love seek the happy knowledge

ledge of their being the sheep of the Lord's pasture, who lack nothing, and who have all manner of things that are good? The great shepherd and bishop of souls watches over them by his almighty power, suffering nothing to hurt them in their real interest, but ordering all things for their benefit. His very judgments upon the wicked are mercies to them. And since he can thus make outward calamities work for their good, what must his acts of grace and love be? Who can tell, how blessed the man is whose iniquities are forgiven, and whose sins are covered? Who has joy and peace in believing that he is pardoned and justified, who has the spirit of adoption in his heart, enabling him to cry, Abba, Father, and abiding with him to strengthen, to comfort, and to sanctify him, shedding daily more and more of the love of God abroad in his heart, and making him fit and meet for glory. Must not such a man be blessed indeed! Can you conceive a more happy state on this side of heaven? And do you not then desire it? If you do, O come, taste, and see what happiness this great and good shepherd does bestow, pray to him for the experience of his love and

power

power, and let us join in calling upon him, and saying,

O Lord Jesu Christ, the great shepherd of the sheep, who hast redeemed them by the blood of the everlasting covenant, look down upon this congregation, and be gracious to those who have no desire to know thee to be the shepherd and bishop of their souls. Shew them their guilt, convince them of their danger, and enable them with those who are now seeking, to wait upon thee, until thou bring them into thy fold; and there feed them with the bread of God, and support them in all troubles and trials, until death be swallowed up in victory. Oh blessed and adorable Jesus, give this whole congregation the sweet experience of the doctrine we have been considering, and although we have all been as sheep going astray, yet grant we may all return to the shepherd and bishop of our souls, and be happy with him in time and in eternity. So be it, to the honour and glory of Father, Son and Holy Spirit, three persons in one Jehovah, to whom be equal praise and worship, now and for ever. *Amen* and *Amen*.

SERMON V.

Chap. i. Ver. 8.

If thou know not, O thou fairest among women, go thy way forth by the footsteps of the flock, and feed thy kids beside the shepherds tents.

THESE words are an answer to the prayer, which the believers had offered up in the preceding verse. They had tasted of the love of the great and good shepherd, and knew they belonged to his flock, and therefore they intreated him to feed them with the bread of God — Give us this day our daily bread, and to lead them in time of trouble and temptation to a place of refuge and safety. Each of them could thus pray for himself, " Tell me, O thou whom " my soul loveth, where thou feedest, where " thou makest thy flock to rest at noon: for " why should I be as one that turneth aside " by the flocks of thy companions?" Why should I be misled by them? If he followed

the

the flocks of thefe companions he would be turned afide, and confequently they were not true fincere companions of Chrift, but only in name and pretence.

In the words which I have now read we have the fuccefs of this prayer. They contain a gracious anfwer from our Lord Jefus, the great fhepherd and bifhop of fouls. The prayer confifted of two parts, and he makes a reply to each. " If thou know not, fays " he, O thou faireft among women, go thy " way forth by the footfteps of the flock," there you will find food, " and feed thy " kids befide the fhepherds tents," there you will find fafety. May his good Spirit enlighten all our underftandings clearly to fee the fenfe of thefe words, and may he enable us to experience the power of them, and if it be his good pleafure by means of what fhall be fpoken.

Firft, In a fhort paraphrafe upon them, and

Secondly, In the practical ufe and application I fhall make of them.

Our blessed Saviour is the great and good shepherd of souls. His greatness makes his goodness more desireable: for he is almighty to give whatever he sees his people want. Whatever they ask of him, he is able and willing to grant it: for he is a God hearing prayer. His ears are always open to receive, his love is always disposed to answer the prayer of faith. So soon as the faithful in the text had sent up their petitions to the great shepherd and bishop of souls, the answer came down. Yea he himself brought it. He that spake and all things were made, he that commanded, and they still obey his commandment and hearken unto the voice of his words, he the God and king of heaven and earth says, *If thou know not,* if thou dost not clearly and fully know, but comest to me for direction and assistance, *O thou fairest among women.* The soul is here spoken of, as the church often is under the similitude of a woman, and said to be fair, fair even in the eyes of Christ, the bridegroom of the church. And by what means was she made thus lovely in his sight? In herself she was black and sinful, and there is nothing so filthy and abominable in the sight of the all-pure God, as sin. He cannot behold the

the least iniquity, and mankind is conceived and born in iniquity, and by nature subject to the wrath of God, how then can he behold it with approbation? Not until it be cleansed from all sin in the blood of the Lamb. When it is justified by his righteousness, and cloathed with his graces, then it will be indeed fair and beautiful; yea perfect through my comeliness, which I had put upon thee, saith the Lord God. When Christ has thus presented the soul to himself not having spot or wrinkle, or any such thing, but holy and without blemish, then he speaks to her as perfect in beauty, " If thou know not, O " thou fairest among women, go thy way " forth by the footsteps of the flock." The great shepherd has but one flock. Although it consists of a great multitude, which no man could number, yet they have but one spirit in them all, but one Lord, one faith, and one baptism. They are of one heart, and of one mind; they walk by the same rule, and mind the same thing. Though part of them be already entered into rest, and others are still in the world, yet they have sweet fellowship and communion with each other in the unity of the spirit. And e'er long they will be all gathered into one place.

There

There will be but one fold, and one shepherd: for in the dispensation of the fulness of times God will gather together in one all things in Christ, both which are in heaven, and which are on earth, even in him.

And as the flock is one, so is the way. There never was but one way, in which the Lord's flock walked. In the same good old way, they that are gone before, and we that are following after them must walk. Many disputes indeed have been raised about it by men who are gone out of the way. The philosophers of *Greece* and *Rome* sought by the light of nature, but could not find it, and our modern reasoners are seeking it by the same light, and still miss it; but believers are at no loss, because their Lord ended all disputes about it, when he declared, " I am the way." He is the only way, because no sinner can come to the Father but by him. You must walk with him in his way, if ever you be reconciled to the Father, and see his face with joy. And what is it that brings us into his way? Faith, the one faith which unites the believer to Christ, and which is justifying faith, because there is no saving faith but this. You may divide faith
into

into many branches according to its feveral offices, and may give it feveral names, but if it be faving faith it is that which juftifies, which by uniting us to Chrift fets us in the right way, and keeps us in it. And this faith all believers had under the *Old Teftament* difpenfation, as certainly as we have it under the *New*. They proved that they had the one faith, by the actings of their faith, as St. *Paul* has taught us at large in the 11th chapter to the *Hebrews*; wherein he fets before us the moft celebrated perfonages in fcripture, and fhews what great things their faith enabled them to do and to fuffer, in order to encourage us to follow the fteps of their faith.

Some perhaps may enquire, whether the faith that juftified and faved them was the fame that we have now: the apoftle replies that there is but *one faith*, and if theirs was not the one faith, how could he propofe their faith to us, and exhort us to follow them, looking, as they did, unto Jefus the author and finifher of faith? Our reformers have confidered the 11th chapter to the *Hebrews* in the fecond part of their homily upon faith, and they fum it up in thefe words:—
" This

" This is the christian faith which these
" holy men had, and we also ought to have.
" And although they were not named chris-
" tian men, yet was it a christian faith that
" they had, for they looked for all benefits
" of God the Father, through the merits of
" his Son Jesus Christ, as we now do. This
" difference is between them and us, that
" they looked when Christ should come;
" and we be in the time, when he is come:
" therefore saith St. *Augustine*, the time is
" altered and changed, but not the faith."
In effect they and we be all one; we have
the same faith that they had, and they the
same that we have, and therefore in the text
we are directed to follow their faith, and
more especially the actings of their faith,
" Go thy way forth by the footsteps of the
" flock." You may see in what way they
walked by the marks and prints of their
feet, which they have left behind them.
Observe those, and tread in their steps. See
what great things, how impossible to flesh
and blood, their faith enabled them to perform, and go and do thou likewise. St.
Paul has determined, that this is the meaning of treading in their steps, in *Rom.* iv. 12.
where he is speaking of *Abraham*'s being
the

the father of all those who tread in the steps of that faith, which he had, being yet uncircumcised — he is the father of all those who can tread in the steps of his faith, who follow him in the actings of his faith, and can give such marks of its sincerity as he did.

Try yourselves then, my brethren, in this point, and examine whether you are following the footsteps of the flock. Can you tread in the steps of *Abraham*'s faith? When God called *Abraham* to leave his country and his father's house, he obeyed, and he went out not knowing whither he went: God does call you to leave the world, and the things of it, and to set your affections upon the things above; and can you, have you obeyed? Do you live in the world, like *Abraham*, a stranger and a pilgrim, knowing that here is not your home, but that you have a better country, namely a heavenly, provided for you? Can you live upon the promises of God, as *Abraham* did, when all things make against you, and rely with full trust and confidence upon the divine faithfulness and truth? Can you give up the dearest object of your heart, be it an only child,

if

if the God of all grace and love should think proper to take it from you? Are you thus strong in faith, giving glory to God? Can you copy after these actings of *Abraham*'s faith? If you cannot follow his steps, consider what is the reason. Do you desire it? If you do, have you not the promise of the same grace which *Abraham* had, to enable you to walk by faith and not by sight? Are not all things possible to him that believeth? Why then are you behind *Abraham?* Oh hasten your steps, and get to the head of the flock. Let none be before you. You have the very same help that the father of the faithful had, therefore cast aside every weight, and the sin which does so easily beset you, (it is sin that stops your course) and press toward the mark, for the prize of the high calling of God in Christ Jesus.

But perhaps some person may ask, where shall I meet with the footsteps of the flock of Christ? Where are there any marks of them to be found? That you might not be at a loss, God has been pleased to leave a lively and exact print of them in the scripture. There you have an impression of all the footsteps, which you are to follow: for the

the word is a lanthorn unto our feet, and a light unto our paths, to guide our feet into the way of peace, and then to order our steps in it. St. *Paul*, 1 Cor. x. having drawn the great outlines of the *Jewish* history, says, " That all these things happened unto them " for examples, and they are written for our " admonition." And having, *Heb.* xi. described the actings of the faith of the *Old Testament* saints, he applies them to us for our example, exhorting us to follow their faith; and he also proposes himself for a pattern to the *Corinthians*, " Be ye followers of me, even " as I also am of Christ"—follow my steps so far as I follow Christ's. In this light we are to consider the footsteps of the flock. Christ is at the head, and goes before his flock, they follow him and tread in his steps, and we who come after tread in theirs, following them in the way, wherein they followed Christ. And all this is recorded for our use in scripture. We are to take no step, unless we see some marks of the flock's having gone before, and taken that very step; and when we are united by faith to Christ, and under the guidance of his good Spirit, we shall then see directions left in scripture, for every step we are to take.
And

And thus though it be not in man that walketh to direct his steps, yet the Lord will hold up our goings in his paths that our footsteps slip not: for the steps of a good man are ordered by the Lord, and he maketh his way acceptable to himself.

This is I think the sense of the first part of my text, namely, of treading in the footsteps of the flock: the next words have very little difficulty, " and feed thy kids beside " the shepherds tents." These shepherds are the servants of the chief shepherd, whose own the sheep are. The ministers of the Lord who have the care and charge of his flock are throughout the scriptures called pastors or shepherds. And their tents here mentioned are not such tents as earthly shepherds pitch, when they are watching their flocks, but certain stated fixed dwellings, wherein they officiated as spiritual pastors and shepherds. The original word is not what our translators commonly render tents, but another which always signifies to dwell or to inhabit, and which is of the same root with *Shecinah*, the habitation of the divine glory in the tabernacle and temple. The first time it occurs is in the third of *Genesis*, where

where the ufe and defign of the cherubim is mentioned—" And God drove out the "man, and he *placed*, he dwelt in, or in- "habited the cherubim." We read of God's appearing in the moft holy place of the tabernacle and temple over the cherubim; for which reafon St. *Paul* calls them the cherubim of glory. And the whole tabernacle and temple, including the holy as well as the moft holy place, with all their facred veffels and apparatus, are generally called by the fame word that is in my text, *viz. the dwelling*. Indeed it is commonly tranflated *tabernacle*, but it fignifies the dwelling-place of the God of *Ifrael*, the place where he had put his name to dwell there. And accordingly when the tabernacle and temple were reared up, the glory of the Lord, that glorious and divine perfon who was the reality of all their types and ceremonies, came and filled them. And it was upon account of his prefence in them, that the faithful could fay, " Lord, I have loved the habita- " tion of thine houfe, and the place where " thy glory dwelleth." Thefe circumftances may lead us to confider the dwellings, mentioned in my text, as places appropriated to a religious ufe, dwellings facred rather than

K. civil,

civil, such as the shepherds dwelt in, when they were acting in their office as pastors over the flock of Christ. In these dwellings they resided in order to dispense the word and the sacraments, and to administer the ordinances to the Lord's people, and to the sheep of his pasture: for here they were to feed the kids; the original word is used for the young of the sheep as well as of the goats; for whom the chief shepherd has a particular love and tenderness. He carries them in his bosom. And they lay near the heart of all the Lord's faithful pastors, who watch with the greatest care over the young and weak part of their flock, using every likely means to preserve and strengthen them, and withal striving much for them with God in prayer. No tender parent can be more concerned for the health of a weak and sickly child, than they are for the weak in the faith. Knowing to what temptations they are exposed, and what difficulties they have to encounter, they labour earnestly to keep them near the shepherds dwellings, in close attendance upon the ordinances, for here they will be safe from danger, and will find food to strengthen their hearts, and to enable them to grow in grace.

I hope

I hope it now appears from what has been said, that the Lord's anfwer is direct and full to his people's prayer. They had defired to learn where he fed his flock, and where he made them reſt in times of great trials and troubles. He replies, with lips full of grace, If thou art at a loſs, O my beloved, whom I have purchaſed with mine own blood, and made fair and lovely with mine own righteouſneſs, go thy way forth by the footſteps of the flock, fee in what way they have always walked, mark the actings of their faith, imitate them, and you will find the more you act faith the ſtronger it will grow. If temptations are powerful, and troubles many and heavy, and the heat of perſecution rages, and faith is ready to ſhrink back, and to give way, then keep near the ſhepherds dwellings. There are the ordinances, upon which in time of danger young and weak believers ſhould attend cloſely. The more they wait upon the Lord with the paſtors of his flock, the more food they will get for their ſouls, and the greater ſafety and ſtrength will they find: for where can the believer hope to grow ſtronger in grace than under the means of grace? Theſe are the inſtituted means of making believers ſtrong in the Lord,

Lord, and in the power of his might, able to withstand in the evil day, and having done all to stand, resisting unto blood, striving against sin.

This is the doctrine of the text, in which there are two rules laid down for the conduct of believers. At all times they are to tread in the footsteps of the flock, and to follow the actings of their faith, and in troublesome times they are to keep near the shepherds dwellings, that they may receive comfort and strength from the use of the ordinances. These are Christ's own directions to them that are in the faith. As to those persons, who have never seen their want of faith and are not seeking it, they are not concerned in what has been said. They have no lot nor share with us in this matter: for how should they follow the footsteps of the flock, who are not yet got into the way in which the flock walks? All men by nature have turned aside from the right way, they have erred and strayed from the ways of God like lost sheep, and have neither will nor power to turn into it. While they are in this state, they don't belong to Christ's flock, and therefore how should they

follow

follow the actings of their faith, who themselves have no faith? My brethren, are any of you in this state? Do you know nothing of your having received faith from God as his gift, and wrought in your heart by the operation of his Spirit? Then you should fear and tremble for your guilt and your danger. Consider your guilt. You have all your sins, original and actual to answer for, and before a God who is of purer eyes than to behold the least iniquity. Consider your danger. Have you not read, " He that be- " lieveth not shall be damned," and are you not afraid of damnation? For while your sins are unpardoned every step you take tends to hell beneath. And what is there between you and it? Think how near you are to it. There is nothing but this thin partition of flesh, and this little vapour of life, this light air that you breathe, nothing else keeps you out of everlasting burnings. And if God was to take away your breath this moment, Oh where would your poor soul be? Meditate on an eternity of torments, and while there is a moment left, use it, and flee from the wrath to come. Flee to Jesus, the great and good shepherd, and try, whether he will not save thee, for there is salvation in none other.

other. If thou art fenfible of thy guilt and of thy danger, fear not. Apply to him, and he will get himfelf glory in bringing thee home to God, and in making thee one of the fheep of his pafture.

Although the directions in the text relate only to the faithful, yet I could not help fpeaking a word to thofe who neither have, nor are feeking, the true faving faith. I pray God to make it ufeful to their fouls, and I now come to apply the firft rule here laid down. It is an anfwer to the prayer of the faithful. They had intreated Chrift to inform them, where he fed his flock; his anfwer is, Go thy way forth by the footfteps of the flock, fee in what way they were led and fupported, and what prints and marks they left behind them, thefe follow, and you will be carried fafe through, as they were. Chrift himfelf is the way, faith fets believers in it by uniting them to Chrift, the footfteps are the actings of faith recorded in fcripture, the great things which by faith the faints of old were enabled to perform, and thefe things the fcripture holds out to us for our example, and admonition. Now my baethren, when you read of the power of

faith

faith in former times, do you find it as powerful in you? Faith is the same: for there is but one faith, and one Lord who gives it, he changeth not, he is the same yesterday, to-day, and for ever. His promises are like himself, truth itself, and unchangeable. Why then is not faith as mighty in operation as it ever was? Why does it not perform the same wonders now, which it did formerly? In the 11th of the *Hebrews* we read of many signal victories, which the old saints obtained by the power of faith, and our church says (second part of the homily upon faith) " St. *Paul* so much extolleth
" their faith, because we should not less, but
" rather more, give ourselves wholly unto
" Christ, both in profession and living, now
" when Christ is come, than the old fathers
" did before his coming. And by all the
" declarations of St. *Paul* it is evident, that
" the true, lively, and Christian faith is no
" dead, vain, or unfruitful thing, but a
" thing of perfect virtue, of wonderful ope-
" ration or working, and strength, bringing
" forth all good motions and good works."
When you read of the actings of faith in former times, try yourselves, my beloved brethren, and see whether it has the same won-

derful operation and working in you. Try whether you can follow the footsteps of the flock. The victories of their faith are marked out for your example, can you then with them triumph over all the enemies of faith, over sin and satan, the world and the flesh, death and the grave? These are the enemies with whom you are to fight the good fight of faith; and these the faithful have defeated. Their faith conquered sin by apprehending and applying Christ's righteousness for pardon and justification, and by drawing from his fulness grace for grace to subdue the dominion of sin. And are you growing in grace, and so strong in faith, that when sin puts on its most alluring dress you can with *Joseph* and *Moses* nobly reject its flattering pleasures? When the devil throws his fiery darts at you, have you the shield of faith ready to hold up in your defence, against which the rage and force of his darts is quenched and spent, so that you can say with *Paul*, I have fought the good fight, I have finished my course, I have kept the faith? When the world invites you with its riches and honours, can you with *Abraham* and his descendants live a wanderer and a sojourner upon earth, knowing that God is
your

your God, and that he hath provided for you a city not made with hands eternal in the heavens? This is living by faith, and not by sight, and this is the victory that overcometh the world, even our faith. Do you know that the will of the flesh is enmity to the will of God, and therefore can your faith submit to suffer the will of God, and with *Job* to bear it patiently? In short, can you with *Paul* rejoice alike in poverty and riches, in pleasure and pain, in honour and disgrace, yea, can you with him do all things through Christ that strengtheneth you? That is a great word—*all things*—I can do all things. And yet faith can speak it without presumption: for all things are possible to him that believeth. It is possible with *David* to fear no evil, no not when you are going through the valley and shadow of death; yea, faith can with the blessed *Paul* give thanks to God for giving it the victory over death through Jesus Christ our Lord.

These are some of the victories of faith, which it has already attained, and which are recorded in scripture for your imitation. And if you find any of them too hard for you, it is not because faith has lost any of its

its virtue and efficacy, but becaufe you don't put faith upon acting. Faith is still almighty. Set it to work, and try its power, and you will find it can do whatever it has done, and why fhould you doubt of its doing what God has promifed it fhall do? Surely the Lord's hand is not fhortened. He can ftill make faith as victorious as it ever was: for he left thefe great exploits of faith upon record for your ufe. Thefe footfteps of the flock were left on purpofe for your encouragement, that you might fee how poffible it was to conquer fin and fatan, the world and the flefh, death and the grave. Thefe are your Lord's enemies as well as yours. It is for his honour that you fhould conquer them. And he promifes you his help, the fame help which he gave to thefe faithful foldiers, who having fought the good fight of faith now ftand confirmed in blifs, with crowns of eternal glory upon their heads, and palms of victory in their hands. Is it not a privilege to be enabled to tread in their fteps? Can there be a greater privilege? Can there be greater happinefs, than to conquer and to be crowned with them? · Oh difparage not then your Lord nor his gifts, by doubting of the power of faith? Fear
not,

not, only believe. Bring your belief into act. Oppose it to your enemies, and see whether it will not make you more than conquerors over them. Whatever God has promised faith should do in you, and for you, is he not almighty to perform? Doubt not then whenever you are following the footsteps of the flock, but his omnipotence will be present with you to fulfil his promises, and you will find that all things are possible to him that believeth.

These victories indeed may be attained by them that are strong in faith—but perhaps some of you may fancy, I am weak in the faith—I must not aspire to such great things. Why not? Faith is the gift of God. And it is mighty by *his* operation. Faith does not work in the strength of nature, but in the omnipotence of grace. And grace is free—as free for you who are a weak believer, as for the strongest. So that you may aspire to great things. Put your faith upon acting, and see whether it will not make you equal to the greatest things: For

Allowing you are weak at present, yet it is not God's intention, that you should
continue

continue so. He has appointed the means of grace for your growth in grace. Attend upon the ordinances, keep near the shepherds dwellings, and there you will find yourselves strengthened and established: for there is food for your soul. God has promised that his quickening Spirit shall be in the ordinances, and that he will render them effectual for the ends for which they were instituted. It is his grace that animates and enlivens them: for without it they are but dead letters, mere carnal ordinances, which profit nothing to the edifying of the soul, but when he quickens them with his divine presence, then they build up and strengthen the believer, and are the means of his growing in grace.

If then any of you are sensible of your having but weak faith, wait upon God for the strengthening of it. And wait in the ways of his ordinances. In them he has promised to be found of those that seek him. You will find his Spirit present in the word, in prayer, and in the sacrament of the Lord's supper. Keep near to them, and God will give you food for your souls, enabling you in the strength of it to get more power over sin, and to be more alive unto God.

The

The word is expresly said to be the means of spiritual life, *Psalm* cxix. 50. *Thy word hath quickened me:* and it is also the means of the growth of this spiritual life, according to the apostle, " As new born " babes desire the sincere milk of the word, " that ye may grow thereby." But then in order that we may thus grow by the word, faith must be mixed with it — St. *Paul* tells the *Thessalonians*, 1 Epistle *Chap.* ii. 13. " When ye received the word of God " which ye heard of us, ye received it not " as the word of men, but (as it is in truth) " the word of God, which effectually work- " eth also in you that believe." Faith makes it work effectually, and unless faith be mixed and incorporated, as it were, with it, it does not profit: for we are assured that the antient *Jews* had the same gospel preached unto them that we have, but the word preached did not profit them, not being mixed with faith in them that heard it.

If you cannot mix faith with the word preached, so as to find yourself growing in grace and strength, can you pray? Prayer is the appointed means of receiving a supply of all your wants, from the fulness of Christ Jesus. Ask and ye shall have, all that he

has

has purchased, and all that he has to give: for his promise is very extensive, *Matt.* xxi. 22. *All things,* without any exception, *whatsoever ye shall ask in prayer believing,* if faith has any ground in the word of promise to believe, that it shall receive what it asks, *ye shall receive it.* Encouraged by this promise, ask humbly whatever God has promised to give. Do you find yourself unable to follow the footsteps of the flock? Cannot you keep near the shepherds tents? But are you drawn away from attending upon the ordinances by the manifold temptations of sin and satan, of the world and the flesh? Pray for power to fight against these enemies, and Christ will make you more than conqueror. The more you pray, the stronger you will grow. Out of weakness you shall be made strong. And by waiting constantly upon the Lord you shall renew your strength, strength to mortify sin, and strength to be alive unto God: yea, by waiting upon God you will receive the fulness of joy; for thus has the God that heareth prayer encouraged you to pray always and not to faint—" Ask and you " shall receive, that your joy may be full." And

Where should we wait upon God for the renewing of our strength and for the fulness
of

of joy, but at his own table? Has not the Lord appointed that his body should be meat indeed, and that his blood should be drink indeed, being the true spiritual food and strengthening of our souls. Our reformers certainly looked upon the Lord's Supper in this light; for to the question in the *Catechism*, "What are the benefits whereof we "are partakers thereby?" they have given this answer, "The strengthening and re- "freshing of our souls by the body and blood "of Christ, as our bodies are by the bread "and wine. The elements are the instituted signs of that life, which Christ purchased by the offering of his body, and by the shedding of his blood. They are signs to all who understand their meaning, but seals to those persons only who are united to Christ by faith, and grafted as branches into the true vine. Wait upon him then, my brethren, in the appointed means for the continuance and growth of this divine life. Be found obedient to his command — Eat this bread and drink of this cup — Do this in remembrance of me, and you will receive something more at the Lord's table, than mere signs. In the bread you will by faith partake of the body, and in the cup you

will

will partake of the blood of Chrift, adminiftering to your foul that divine life, which he begins here in grace, and carries on for ever and ever in glory.

These are the inftituted means in which the weak in faith ought to wait upon the Lord, and he has encouraged them to wait upon him in thefe means with a promife, that he will therein be found of them that feek him, and will ftrengthen and eftablifh their hearts in the faith. We are his witneffes, that he is faithful and juft to fulfil his promifes. We atteft this upon our own experience. We found ourfelves growing in grace by attendance upon the ordinances. We expected to receive freely what God had freely promifed, and we are not difappointed of our hope. And this will be your happy experience, my brethren, who are now endeavouring to follow the footfteps of the flock. Keep near the fhepherds tents. Attend clofe upon the ordinances, and you will grow ftrong in the Lord, and in the power of his might. And when you are ftrong, beware of fpiritual pride. Beware of being drawn away from the ordinances, as if they were not as neceffary for you now, as they were formerly. Remember that you ftand in the
Lord's

Lord's strength, and he expects you should wait upon him for the continuance of it. And if you leave off attending upon the ordinances, because you think you are strong in faith, it is just as if a strong man should fancy he had no occasion to eat any more, because of his great strength. Our souls want continual supplies of grace, as our bodies stand in need of daily bread. And God has promised to make the ordinances food for his children, and he daily fulfils his promises to them. They find the quickening Spirit in the ordinances, communicating to them life and comfort and strength, according to their several wants and necessities.

And as if these were not sufficient motives to encourage you to wait upon God in the ways of his ordinances, he has promised to do more for those who wait therein, than they can either ask or think: " For since " the beginning of the world men have not " heard, nor perceived by the ear, neither " hath the eye seen, O God, besides thee, " what he hath prepared for him that waiteth " for him. Thou meetest him that rejoiceth, " and worketh righteousness, those that re- " member thee in thy ways." (*Isaiah* lxiv. 4, 5.) Let us then remember God in his ways,

ways, and in thefe ways he will meet us with a bleffing. Whatever he has promifed, he will certainly fulfil. Wait upon him and you fhall not be afhamed. Follow the flock, and you fhall be fafe. Follow them, as they followed Chrift, and you will be kept as they were. And let us look up to him for his gracious help to enable us to follow the fteps of their faith, humbly praying to him in the words of our church, and faying —

"O almighty God, who haft knit to-
"gether thine elect in one communion and
"fellowfhip, in the myftical body of thy
"Son Chrift our Lord; grant us grace fo
"to follow thy bleffed faints in all virtuous
"and godly living, that we may come to
"thofe unfpeakable joys, which thou haft
"prepared for them that unfeignedly love
"thee, hrough Jefus Chrift our Lord.
"Amen." *Collect for All Saint's Day.*

SERMON VI.

Chap. iv. Ver. 16.

Awake, O north wind, and come thou south, blow upon my garden, that the spices thereof may flow out.

IN the foregoing chapter the believing soul had been in a dull heavy frame, but being concerned and uneasy about it, had desired the quickening influences of Christ's grace. Christ here answers these desires. He calls for the wind to come and blow upon his garden. The wind is the scripture emblem and representative of the Holy Spirit. When he descended upon the disciples on the day of *Pentecost*, he came in this his known emblem, in a rushing mighty wind, and it follows, " they were " all filled with the Holy Ghost," filled with his gifts and graces. For the same good purpose his influence is here required. He is to blow upon the garden with his several operations, to quicken those things, that were ready to die, and to bring forth the sweet perfumes of the graces of his own planting. " Awake, O north wind, and come thou south — blow upon my garden, that the spices thereof may flow out." May the enlivening Spirit bring the sweet experience of these words to all your hearts. As he is the omnipresent God, he is here with us; Oh that he may be present in these his gracious offices. Like the sharp penetrating north wind may he awaken conviction, and then come like the mild and soft south wind with his comforts, that he may plant his graces in us, and cause the spices of them to flow out. God grant these may be the happy effects of our considering

First, The sense and meaning of the words.

Secondly, Of our defending the doctrine contained in them. And

Thirdly, Of our applying them to our spiritual use and benefit.

And *First*, Let us consider the sense of the words. Christ is the speaker. He had been

been comparing the church to a garden, which he had enclosed from the wilderness of the world. He had taken it in for his own use, and had set in it trees of righteousness, which he had moved out of the common waste, where they grew wild by nature, and had transplanted them into his garden. The faithful are the trees, which the heavenly husbandman sets in his own paradise. And by his cultivation, by being watered with his grace, and by clear shining after rain, from being wild and barren by nature they are changed, and they become trees of righteousness, the planting of the Lord, that he may be glorified: For here" in, says the blessed Jesus, is my Father " glorified, that ye bring forth much fruit." The Lord has no barren trees in his paradise. Before he transplanted them they were a seminary of all evil weeds, they brought forth nothing that was good; but when once set in his garden they had a new spirit put into them, from whence come the seeds of all graces. For thus Christ in this chapter describes his garden. Its plants are an orchard of pomegranates, with pleasant fruits, camphire with spikenard — spikenard and saffron, calamus and cinnamon, with all trees of frankincenſe, myrrh and aloes, with all the chief ſpices. Upon this garden thus enriched like the paradiſe of God he calls the wind to blow, that it might bring forth the fragrancy of all its chief ſpices. The wind is the agent, that was to make them flow out. And wind is air in motion — air in action. This was the firſt mover in the formation of the world, and it is ſtill the principal mover in the formation and growth of every tree and plant. Natural hiſtorians have lately demonſtrated by undoubted experiments, that none of them can live without air. They want it as much as animals do. By it the odoriferous kind diffuſe their fragrancy. The air is the cauſe that firſt draws out, and then ſpreads abroad their ſweet perfumes. And by it the fruit-bearing kind will ſoon be adorned with beautiful bloſſoms, and in their ſeaſon with rich and ripe fruit. Their vegetable life with all the operations of it depends upon the air, in like manner as our ſpiritual life with all the operations of it depends upon the Holy Spirit, of whom the air was the inſtituted type. In our preſent embodied ſtate we cannot ſee ſpiritual, but through the glaſs of material objects. We are confined to ſenſe. And therefore God has been pleafed to make ufe of fenfible things in nature to reprefent the fpiritual things in grace. He has drawn a juft and perfect parallel. In the works of creation he has given us an expreffive image of every fpiritual object, with which he faw it needful for us to be accquainted. Of himfelf, of his effence, of his perfonality, and of the offices of the divine perfons in the œconomy of the covenant, he has fet before our eyes in the agency of nature a lively picture: for the grand agent in nature is the air, which is one in effence, whether it be rarified to its fmalleft parts in the action of fire at the orb of the fun, or fent out in light, or returned in grofs air to maintain and carry on this action of fire at the orb of the fun, in which foever of thefe three diftinct operations it be imployed it is ftill air: and accordingly this unity of its effence, and diftinction of its threefold agency, is declared in fcripture to be the inftituted type, in which we are to read the unity of the divine effence and the offices of the three divine perfons. The *Pfalmift* referring to the created image fays, *The heavens declare the glory* of God.— The heavens are not empty fpace, for that could declare nothing, but they are the air in its three diſtinct offices, each of which is a record of God's glory. For as the apoſtle explains the point, " The inviſible things of " God are clearly ſeen from the creation of " the world," the inviſible things themſelves cannot be ſeen, but they may be ſeen by the creation, " and underſtood by the things " that are made, even his eternal power and " Godhead." So that there is a picture in the things which are made, whereby we may underſtand the things of God which are not made. And this picture, ſo far as I am concerned to explain it at preſent, is the threefold agency of the air, in which are repreſented the offices of the three divine agents in carrying on the work of ſalvation. The covenant itſelf, and the diſtinct offices of the perſons, were for the equal glory of each. It pleaſed the Father to get glory to the divine juſtice and holineſs by demanding full ſatisfaction for ſin. — He was the avenger of ſin, and therefore air in the action of fire is his emblem: he is called in ſcripture a conſuming, a devouring fire, and a jealous God. It pleaſed the Son to get glory to the divine love and mercy by paying this ſatiſfaction, and therefore his conſtant name in ſcripture is light, which is the life of the

material

material world, as he is the life of the spiritual world. And it pleased the Eternal Spirit to get glory to all the divine attributes by inspiring dead sinners with a desire to be raised to newness of life, and then by breathing it into their souls, and carrying it on through the life of grace until he bring them to the life of glory, and therefore he knows no other name in scripture than spirit, or air in motion. The very same word that stands for the breath we breathe, both in the Hebrew and Greek, signifies the Holy Spirit. Why was this the usage of scripture? Was it from the poverty of these languages? No. It was to shew us the perfect likeness and resemblance there is between what air does to the body, and what the Holy Spirit does to the soul. He is the breath of its life. Our souls can no more live to God, without his grace, than our bodies can without air. And after we have received his grace, are quickened and made alive by it, we want its influence every moment to support and to carry on the life which he has given, in like manner as we want breath every moment to support and to carry on our animal life; without it the body can do no work — without his grace

the

the foul can do none. The neceffity of his continually breathing into our fouls the breath of life, is beautifully reprefented in the text. He is there defcribed under his known emblem, wind or air in motion, and what air is to the trees of the garden, that is he to the fpirits of men. Both are alike neceffary. Nothing can grow in the garden without air, neither can any grace grow in our fouls unlefs the Holy Spirit act in thefe his two offices. *Awake, O north wind, and come thou fouth wind.* The fun is never in the northern point of the heavens, and therefore the north wind is cold, fharp, and piercing — But the fun is always in the fouth, and therefore the fouth wind is of a contrary quality, being warm, foft and comforting — the influences of both are neceffary. The north wind was to awake. It was to be the firft mover: the Holy Spirit was to begin in this office. For all men lay in the dead fleep of fin, without the leaft motion of fpiritual life, until the Holy Spirit awaken them. And his general method of awakening finners is to infpire them with conviction of fin. He opens their eyes, fhews them their guilt, and lets them fee their danger. And this is very painful and diftreffing, and therefore it

is

is compared to the north wind, which in the firſt work of grace awakens and acts with all the ſharpneſs of conviction upon the ſinners heart. Here Chriſt calls it to act upon the faithful members of his church, not to bring them into the deep diſtreſs which perſons under conviction of ſin are commonly in, but to preſerve in them a lively ſenſe of their own inſufficiency, and of their dependance upon him. This is neceſſary to keep them always humble, and to make them always ready to aſcribe the glory of what God has done in them to the riches of his free grace. And therefore we find that the Holy Spirit works this temper in all the faithful. None have ſuch clear humbling views of themſelves as they have, which empty them of ſelf, and diſpoſe them to receive more and more of the ſweet influences of the Holy Spirit. And theſe are here deſcribed under the character of the ſouth wind — gentle, and mild, and comforting. It is obſervable, that the ſouth wind was not to awake, but to come — the ſinner muſt be awakened, and convinced of his guilt and danger before he is comforted. This is God's method of acting. His good Spirit firſt makes men feel how miſerable

they

they are without a Saviour, and then he gives them the comfort of knowing their intereſt in him. He awakes and blows upon them like the ſharpeſt blaſts of the pinching north wind, and then he comes with the comfortable breathings of the gentle ſouth. Both theſe are neceſſary: for Chriſt calls for both to blow upon his garden. The original word here rendered *to blow*, is tranſlated in the 2d chapter of *Geneſis*, *to breath* — when ſpoken of God's infuſing an immortal ſpirit into the body of *Adam*. " And the " Lord God formed the man of the duſt of " the ground, and *breathed* into his noſtrils " a ſoul of lives." *Elihu* aſcribes this to the Holy Spirit, as an œconomical act of his office, *Job* xxxiii. 4. " The Spirit of God " hath made me, and the breath of the Almighty hath given me life." In the very ſame manner our Lord repreſented the operation of the Holy Spirit, *John* xx. 22. " He " breathed on his diſciples and ſaid, receive " ye the Holy Ghoſt," he breathed on them to denote by this outward and viſible ſign, the inward and ſpiritual breathing of the Holy Spirit, which he then gave them. Our ſouls are not alive to God, until he infuſe into them this divine breath, as you may read

read at large in the parable of the dry bones, *Ezek.* xxxvii. And his continual breathing upon the faithful foul is as neceffary as this firft act, and therefore it is fpoken of in the text by the fame word. " Breathe with " every gracious influence, O divine Spirit, " upon my faithful people, that the fpices " in them may flow out." The fpices are certainly the graces of Chrift, which he freely beftows upon us who are united to him the head of life and influence, and which are quickened and exercifed by his good Spirit. And when he enables us to bring them into continual ufe and practice, then they become an odor of a fweet fmell, a facrifice acceptable, well pleafing unto God.

The words thus explained offer thefe particulars to our ferious confideration. *Firft,* We are here reminded of the ftate in which all men are while they continue in the barren defolate wildernefs of nature. *Secondly,* We learn by what means Chrift's people are tranfplanted out of the wildernefs into the garden of the Church, where they grow and flourifh; and *thirdly,* the caufe is defcribed that makes the fpices in them to flow out, and enables them to bring forth fruit unto ever-

everlasting life. These are the great truths contained in the text, which I am under my second general head to defend from the authority of God's word.

And first, our state by nature is not a state of grace. We are not born in the garden of the church, but in the wilderness of the world, in a dry barren land, where no water is — no dew nor rain, no kindly influence of heaven, to make us grow in grace. In this barren soil we are like the wild olive tree — we bear no fruit, until the heavenly husbandman move us, and graft us contrary to nature into the good olive tree: for you know it is contrary to nature to graft a wild scion upon a good stock, it is against the common practice in all other trees but the olive. And therefore the apostle, *Rom.* xi. uses this instance to represent the taking of the *Gentiles* into the church of God. The wild olive, like man in his natural state, bears no fruit, but when he is grafted like the wild scion upon the good olive, then he bears forth fruit abundantly. He can bear no fruit of himself: for our blessed Saviour, speaking of the branches not bearing fruit, except they abide in the stock upon which they

they were grafted, declares, No more can ye except ye abide in me, for without me ye can do nothing. In yourselves you are like the ground, which was cursed for your sakes, and which naturally brings forth nothing but thorns and thistles.

When the Holy Spirit first begins to move in our hearts, he convinces us of these truths. He lets us see how barren we are by nature, and unfruitful. He shews us that in us dwelleth no good thing, and that we have nothing but sin in ourselves — He makes us feel the burden of our sins — It presseth us sore, and forceth us to cry out earnestly for deliverance; when he has thus like the north wind, pierced us with the sharpness of conviction, then is he ready to administer comfort, by transplanting us out of the wilderness into the garden of his church, where, under his mild influence we may grow and flourish; and this is the second doctrinal point in the text worthy of our consideration.

We cannot transplant ourselves, any more than a tree in a bad soil can transplant itself into a good one. But all the faithful are

the

the trees of the Lord's planting. They are taken out of the wildernefs, and removed into the paradife of God, where they are fet, that they may be called trees of righteoufnefs, the planting of the Lord, that he may be glorified in their bearing much fruit. The whole work of bringing us from a barren to a fruitful ftate, from a bad foil to a good one, is the Lord's. It is he who maketh us to be like a tree planted by the waterfide, that will bring forth his fruit in due feafon, his leaf alfo fhall not wither, and look, whatfoever he doth it fhall profper. As it is the action of the air, which firft begins and afterwards carries on the vegetable life in every tree and plant — fo is it the action of the Spirit which firft begins and afterwards carries on fpiritual life. We fhould not even have a defire for it, unlefs he put it into our hearts, and the carrying of it on is the continuance of his work, as much as the life of a tree depends on the continuance of the action of the air upon it: for we are helplefs and without ftrength either to begin or to carry on fpiritual life, but as we are endued with power from on high. All the work is the Lord's: for it is he who worketh in us both to will and to do.

Now

Now it is the fame hand, which firft plants us, that afterwards waters us with the dew of his heavenly grace, and makes us fruitful. This is the third doctrinal point in the text. All our graces come from the Holy Spirit. He firft plants them in us, and then makes the fpices of them to flow out. We cannot doubt of thefe truths, becaufe we have often affented to them, when we repeated the *Nicene Creed*. I wifh we had all experienced the truth of the words—" I " believe in the Holy Ghoft the Lord and " giver of life"—he is the Lord and giver of all fpiritual and divine life. The life itfelf, whereby we live unto God, and all the offices of it, worketh in us that one and the felf-fame Spirit, dividing unto every man his own gifts, as he will. His own gifts are all the graces of the chriftian life. Faith, hope, love, with every fweet and heavenly temper are his gifts: for they are called the fruits of the Spirit. Sin is our own. Our foil bears nothing elfe. It grows weeds, thorns and thiftles, without any cultivation. Our earth is a mother to them, but a ftep-mother to every grace. Whatever there is in us befides weeds, is the free gift of the Holy Spirit. Every good thought, and word, and work,

every step we take in our Christian life is from him. And when he has inspired any thing good into us, he does not leave us to ourselves to improve it. No. It is God that giveth the increase. He worketh in us both to will and to do, according to the *Psalmist*'s prayer, " Stablish the thing, O " God, that thou hast wrought in us." He stirs up his own gifts and graces—keeps them in exercise—and makes the spices of them to flow out. When we work in his strength, we work what is well pleasing. God the Father sees us in his Son, partakers of his righteousness, and led by his Spirit, and then the sweet odour of our services ascends with acceptance to the throne of his grace. St. *John* has given us a beautiful image of the manner in which our very best services, even the prayers and praises of God's own people, become acceptable. It is not for any merit in them. It is not because they flow from fervent affections, that they are set before God as incense, and that the lifting up of our hands is an evening sacrifice. But it is through Christ that our very prayers are pleasing unto the Father; for thus we read—*Rev.* viii. 2. " That the angel of " the covenant, our Lord Jesus Christ, came
" and

"and stood at the altar having a golden cen-
"ser, and there was given unto him much
"incense, that he should offer it with the
"prayers of all saints upon the golden altar,
"which was before the throne, and the
"smoke of the incense, which came with
"the prayers of the saints, ascended up
"with acceptance before God out of the
"angel's hand." Here we see that our best prayers are nothing worth unless presented before God by the Redeemer, and perfumed with the sweet incense of his merits. When he presents them before the throne of grace, they then become *his* prayers, and how can the Father deny the requests of his beloved Son? He will answer them, either by giving us what we ask, or something else, that he sees will be much better for us. If then we would profit and be fruitful under the means of grace, if we would have the spices of our prayers and praises and our other religious services to ascend with acceptance before God, let us look up to the Holy Spirit, and intreat him to enable us to apply what has been said to our own hearts. And may he blow upon us with his gracious inspiraraton: while I am in the

Third place, Drawing some practical inferences from what has been said.

The church is here compared to a garden, the faithful to trees of righteousness, which the Lord hath planted, the Holy Spirit to wind, which is to blow upon the trees, and which makes the spices thereof to flow out, as the Holy Spirit brings forth into use and exercise the graces of the faithful. This is the doctrine; and that we may improve by it, let us examine ourselves, whether we are as gardens and trees, whom the Lord hath planted, and in whom he is glorified. Have we been taken out of the wilderness, and transplanted into the paradise of God? Has the Holy Spirit awakened the north wind to convince us of sin, and come with the south wind to comfort us? Has he united us to Christ, engrafted us into the true vine, and do our tender grapes give a pleasant smell? Does he call forth the graces which he has given us, and let the spices of them flow out in daily exercise, so that men seeing our fruitfulness glorify our Father which is in heaven. Happy are they who thus flourish like a palm-tree, and grow like a cedar in *Libanus*. If you be thus happy, my brethren, you cannot

not but know it, and feel it and be thankful to God for it; and to thofe amongſt you who are not in this happy cafe I will make my firſt application. May the Spirit of the living God open your underſtandings to profit from what I have to fay.

If you be not united to Chriſt by faith on your part, and by the bond of the Spirit on Chriſt's part, and thereby enabled to bring forth fruit unto everlaſting life, confider how dangerous your fituation is. There are two fpirits, which divide the world between them: you muſt be led by one or the other, by the Holy Spirit, or by the evil fpirit. And you cannot be at a lofs to know under whofe influence you are. By their fruits ye may know them. This is an infallible mark; which the apoſtle has largely infiſted upon in the 5th chapter of the *Galatians*, where he has given us a defcription at length of the fruits of the Spirit, and of the abominable deeds of the fleſh, which are the fruits of the devil. Read the defcription, and then judge to whom you belong. What flows out of your hearts? What do your tongues delight to be talking of, and your hands to handle, and your feet to run into? What appears in your lives and converfations? Surely you cannot be at a lofs to know what fort of fruit you bear. You cannot be ignorant whether you live to the flefh, or to the Spirit. If you abound in the fruits of righteoufnefs, and the fpices thereof are continually flowing out, a fweet fmelling favour acceptable to God and to all around you, if thus through the Spirit you bear your fruit unto holinefs, then the end will be everlafting life; but if ye live to the flefh, fays God, ye fhall die, die from God and glory, ye fhall die both the firft, and the fecond death.

While you are in this dangerous ftate, how do you keep your confciences quiet? Have you perfuaded yourfelves, that the doctrine is not true? Do you think there is no neceffity for bringing forth the fruits of the Spirit? But remember that you muft be bringing forth fome fruit; and which would you bring forth? Whether, what is pleafing to God, or what is difpleafing? Certainly what is pleafing. And by whofe power and might can you bring it forth? Not by your own. You are by nature helplefs and without ftrength to bring forth any acceptable fruit: for Chrift himfelf fpeaking upon this very

very subject says, "Without me ye can do "nothing." Be persuaded then to apply to him for faith, that ye may be ingrafted into him the true vine, and may bear much and ripe fruit to the glory of God.

But still the doctrine does not appear to you in a clear light. What is the reason? It is because you are in the flesh, in your natural state, and the motions of sin which are by the law do work in your members to bring forth fruit unto death. Sin has such power over you, that you love its dead works, and you hate holiness. You would thank God for making you holy just when you are dying; at the last hour you would like well enough to bring forth fruit unto God, and to have your spices flowing out, but you cannot bear the thoughts of living an holy life. Is not this your case? If it be, is not your faith a dead faith? And how then can you be a living member of Christ; for you were never ingrafted into him the true vine? And if you should be cut off in this state, read your sentence. The God who is to judge you, has already declared—"If a "man abide not in me he is cast forth as a branch, and is withered, and men gather "them,

" them, and caft them into the fire, and
" they are burned." May the Holy Spirit
fet this fcripture home with full conviction
upon your confciences, that you may follow
me with profit in my

Second application, to thofe who are feeking to be united to Chrift, and are defirous of glorifying him by bringing forth much fruit. Examine carefully, my brethren, whether you feek aright. Have you a fingle eye to God's glory? And do you indeed pray, that his will may be done in you; Would you receive Chrift in all his offices? Do you defire him as your king, and would you have his kingdom fet up within you to deftroy in you the reign of fin, as well as your prophet and prieft to fave you from the guilt and punifhment of fin? Are you willing he fhould make you holy as well as happy? If it be the fincere defire of your heart to have the dominion of fin deftroyed in your mortal body, then you may take courage. And if you are alfo fet upon attaining the graces of Chrift, and would have them in ufe and exercife, the fweet fpices of them continually flowing out, then feek, and you fhall find. You have the promifes

of

of God to rely upon, and he cannot deny himself. Seek him with humility in the ways, wherein he has promised to be found of them that seek him. Attend upon him in the ways of the ordinances. In them wait, and be assured, that when it will be for God's glory and your comfort, the Holy Spirit who has already awakened the north wind to convince you of sin, will also come with the mild south wind to refresh and comfort your hearts, and to unite you to Jesus Christ, in whom you may bring forth much fruit. And to those who are in this happy state I make my *third* and last inference.

The faithful in the text desired the Holy Spirit would make them more lively and fruitful. And the faithful still have the same desires, which are at this time more fervent and earnest, because they hear it objected to their most holy faith, that it makes no change in mens lives and conversations: for which reason they pray for more grace, and to have it more in use and exercise, that they may adorn the doctrine of God their Saviour in all things. They would have all men, who see their lives, to behold the great change

change that the Holy Spirit has wrought in them. While they grew in the wildernefs they were like other wild barren trees, but being removed into the garden of the church of Chrift, and become trees of the Lord's planting, they now bear much fruit. And like as the air draws forth the rich fragrancy of the aromatic flowers, and diffufes their fweet odours all around: fo the Holy Spirit keeps in action the graces of the faithful, and makes the fpices thereof to flow out to the glory of God, and to the delight and good of mankind.

Pray then, my chriftian friends and brethren, for the continual influences of the Holy Spirit: thefe are as neceffary for the growth of grace in your foul, as the blowing of the air is to the growth of the fruits of the garden. Convinced of this great truth, and you are convinced of it by happy experience, apply to the Holy Spirit for what you ftand in need of every moment. And pray him to awaken the north wind, whenever its fharp influences are neceffary, either to awaken fecure finners, or to quicken and ftir up the graces of the faithful, and then to come like the fouth wind with his mild

and

and comforting influences, blowing upon the garden, upon the believer, and making the spices thereof, the graces in him, to flow out. And thus may the Holy Spirit enable you and me to experience this scripture in its fullest sense to the glory of God, and to the good of others, and to the comfort of our own souls. May the blessed and adorable Jesus send his good Spirit to lead us all to, and to graft us all into, him the true vine, that we may live unto God, and flourish, and be fruitful. Grant, O gracious Saviour, that every branch in thee, which beareth fruit, may be purged, and may bring forth more fruit, even rich and ripe fruit, which endureth unto everlasting life, to the honour of the holy, blessed, and glorious Trinity, three self-existent persons in one Jehovah, to whom we give equal praise, majesty, and dominion, now and for ever. *Amen*.

SERMON VII.

Chap. v. Ver. 16.

Yea, he is altogether lovely.

THE Holy Spirit puts these words into the mouth of the believer. He has been drawing a character of his beloved Jesus, and has compared him to the most useful and noble objects in the creation, in order to set forth his due praise. But upon reviewing the character he finds it fall short of the perfection of his divine Saviour. It did not come up to the idea which he himself had formed of him, and therefore he finishes in one word, *Yea, he is altogether lovely.* He is all loveliness.—Whatever is lovely and desireable upon earth, whatever is lovely and desireable in heaven—all the graces of time, and all the blessings of eternity, center in him as their proper source, and flow from him as their proper fountain. Whatever can be proposed to the understanding as excellent, whatever the will rightly disposed can desire, whatever the heart and the affections can be set upon and find happiness in, all this is to be met with in the Lord Jesus, and no where else: for *he is altogether lovely*, all beauty, all excellency in himself. And this consideration should endear to us his inherent excellencies, that he is willing to communicate them. This should give a new grace to each, and make it more valuable in our eyes. He is not only altogether lovely, but will also make vile and abominable sinners, when they apply to him for his righteousness, altogether lovely in the sight of God. He will wash them clean from all their sins in his most precious blood, and will clothe them with his all-perfect righteousness, in which they shall appear at the bar of justice without spot of sin unto salvation.

Now since the Lord Jesus is all loveliness, what can be the reason, that he does not appear altogether lovely in the eyes of men? The generality of them see nothing lovely in him. What was formerly said upon the occasion is still true, *Lord, who hath believed our report?* The word of God reports him to be altogether lovely, and the ministers of God preach his loveliness as testified by scripture

scripture and their own experience, but worldly men see no form nor comeliness in him that they should desire him. They see more loveliness in sin, in pleasure, in money, in diversions, than they hope to find in our Lord and Saviour. This dangerous mistake arises either from the judgment or the affections—either they do not see how perfectly lovely Jesus Christ is, or else the affections are prejudiced against him; but wherever the mistake lies, I will offer some scripture arguments to remove it, and may God accompany them with the effectual working of his power, while I am setting before you

First, What Jesus Christ is as man.

Secondly, What he is as God. And

Thirdly, What he is as the incarnate God—as God and man united in one person. And in each of these respects I hope the Holy Spirit will convince you, that Jesus Christ is altogether lovely.

And *First*, Let us view him as man. I mention not his person, though the *Psalmist* says,

ſays, he was fairer than the children of men. The excellencies and endowments of his mind were ſo great and uncommon, that I need not inſiſt on a leſs important part of the ſubject. For conſider, what is it that you admire and love in any perſon? Do extraordinary gifts or graces draw your eſteem? Great abilities or great virtues? Behold every thing that can adorn or dignify the human nature meets in the man Chriſt Jeſus. If true wiſdom and learning be your admiration, it is written, *that in him were laid up all the treaſures of wiſdom and knowledge.* Do you think, that learning never appears ſo graceful, as when it is ſet off with the charms of virtue? Then look upon Jeſus. In him you ſee not this or that particular virtue only, but virtue itſelf in a body of fleſh; and therefore made fleſh, that he might let his graces ſhine before men, and communicate their ſweet influence. He was goodneſs itſelf, and he went about doing good to the ſouls and to the bodies of men, teaching and enlightening the ignorance of their underſtanding, and regulating the depravity of the will and affections, and healing all manner of ſickneſs, and all manner of bodily infirmities. There was not a malady, which ſin had

had brought upon foul or body, but what he proved himself almighty to heal. Was there ever such a character as this? So universally amiable and lovely? Here is a person of all the sons of men the greatest and happiest in himself, and capable of making us great and happy: yea therefore made man, that he might communicate to us his greatness and happiness. And shall any of us be so far lost to all sense of what is great and happy, as not to admire this character? Shall men adore and idolize the true patriot, whose breast burns with love for his country, and who freely hazards his all to save it? And shall the very same men be wanting in esteem for the great patriot of the whole world? How absurd, how inconsistent would this be? What a contradiction is it to throw away all our admiration upon lesser excellencies, and to have none to spare for him, who had every excellency that can adorn the human nature either for beauty or use, and who consequently had every thing that could make him altogether lovely?

If I should stop here, enough has been said to place the man Jesus high above the sons of men; but I have mentioned the least and

and lowest part of his character. He was not only great and good, but had also one thing peculiar to himself, that no sinful frailty or weakness ever sullied his greatness or his goodness. He was a perfect man. You will not find any other character without its spots and blemishes, because there is no man living without sin, our nature itself being sinful, and sin is the cause of all our imperfections. The darkness of the understanding in the things of God comes from sin, and the weakness of the memory, and the continual inclinations of the will to evil, and the strong and unlawful attachment of the heart to the world and to the things of it, spring from the same fountain of sin. But the holy Jesus had no sin, and consequently none of the imperfections which sin has brought upon us. When a truth was proposed to his understanding, there was no obstruction in the faculty; he comprehended it clearly and fully. His will was in harmony with God's will — " I delight, says he, to do thy will, O my God;" and he did it with all his heart, always and perfectly. And accordingly we read of him in the *Psalms*, " That he spake the truth in " his heart," his tongue and his heart always went together — " he had clean hands," not once

once defiled with any sinful pollution — "and a pure heart," not one evil thought had ever arisen in it — nay, "his mind had never been lift up unto vanity," not one vain thought had ever past through his mind. Judge then how perfectly immaculate he must have been: for who is there among us, that has not had a thousand, yea ten thousand vain and wandering thoughts? Who does not find them passing through his mind against his will, and intruding into his hours of devotion, from which he had shut them out, and haunting him even at the Lord's table? But Christ's pure and spotless mind never admitted one vain thought. He was the very image of God, in which the first *Adam* was made, and he did not deface it as the first *Adam* did, but he kept it holy and undefiled. The scripture assures us of it — "He was made sin for us, who knew "no sin." He asserts it of himself — "The "prince of this world cometh, and hath no- "thing in me. Happy for us satan could find in him no part of our fallen image, and therefore the accuser of the brethren could lay no charge against his person, nor consequently against the merit of those actions and sufferings, whereby we, who have by nature

borne

borne the image of the earthy, may through grace bear the image of the heavenly *Adam*, who is the Lord from heaven.

My brethren, weigh and confider this part of our Lord's character. Is he not altogether lovely? And have you then no praife or admiration to beftow upon him? Whatever you fee reafon to admire in any man, if it be indeed praife-worthy, it was in its perfect degree in Chrift Jefus; and therefore certainly you will not with-hold from him his tribute of praife. If your praife follow excellency, behold here is a man not only the chief among ten thoufand, but alfo the chief of the human race. A man that never had his fellow — a perfect man. He has every good gift, and every grace that can be in man. And will you not admire and efteem fuch a character? Does he not appear to you altogether amiable? If you fee any thing wanting in him, it is an argument of your own imperfection: for he, whofe all-fearching eye trieth the very hearts and reins, faw no way of wickednefs in him. He pronounced him to be his beloved Son, in whom he was well pleafed, and he honoured him with a wonderful glory, never communicated to any creature,

creature, but to the man Jesus; he was united to God the Son in so close and intimate an union, that God and man were one Christ, as much as the reasonable soul and flesh are one man. O how great is the mystery of godliness — *God manifest in the flesh!* How can we sufficiently admire and adore it! And how greatly should it endear to us the humanity of our Lord, that it was the sacred temple of the Godhead, inhabited by God the Son, and honoured with the more immediate presence of the Father and the Holy Spirit: for it pleased the Father that in him should all fulness dwell, even the fulness of the Godhead bodily. Surely then the man Jesus was altogether lovely; since he was lovely in the eyes of the eternal Trinity, who vouchsafed to dwell and to make their abode in him. Oh blush then and be ashamed, ye sinful worms who see nothing lovely in Jesus Christ, since the most blessed God sees him altogether lovely. Can ye find no comeliness in *him*, of whom the Father hath said — " This is my be-
" loved Son, in whom I am well pleased."
And are not ye well pleased with him, ye ungrateful men, for whom he was made man? Pardon, Lord Jesus, our low opinion
of

of the dignity of thy human nature. Let thy good Spirit teach us to form more exalted ideas of thee, while I am

Secondly, Speaking of the glory of thy divine nature.

All lovelineſs is certainly in God, inherent in him as the fountain, from whence flows whatever is lovely in the creation. And if Jeſus Chriſt be the true God, then he muſt have every attribute and perfection, that can endear him to his creatures, and make him altogether lovely in their eyes: and that he is the true God is as certain as that there is a God. The ſcripture has given him the names and the attributes of God, and has aſcribed to him the works, which none but the almighty Creator, and the all-wiſe Preſerver of the world could perform. He is called Jehovah, the incommunicable name of the Divine Eſſence, and Immanuel, which being interpreted is, *God with us.* He is ſaid to be omniſcient and omnipreſent, to have created all things, and to uphold them by the word of his power: he came in the fleſh to redeem them, and there is a day at hand, when he will come to judge them,

them. And will any man say, that these are the attributes and works of a creature? Do they not evidently belong to the blessed and only potentate, the King of Kings, and Lord of Lords, of whom the *Old Testament* says, that he is God the Saviour, and that there is none other, as *Isaiah* xlv. 21. 22. " There is " no God else beside me, a just God and a " Saviour, there is none beside me — Look " unto me, and be ye saved all the ends " of the earth: for I am God, and there " is none else." The apostle teaches the same doctrine in the *New Testament*, where he says (*Rom.* ix. 5.) " that Christ is over all " God blessed for ever. Amen.

In these two passages (not to mention others) the Saviour is expressly said to be God — God over all, and consequently he must be altogether lovely; for every perfection which has any claim to our love is inherent in him, and whatever we see of loveliness in the works of nature owes its being to his divine wisdom and power and goodness; so that whenever you see any thing worthy of your admiration, it should lead your thoughts up to Jesus Christ, the almighty creator and preserver of it. If you stop short of him, you rob him of his honour: because

because its loveliness is his. And what then must he be, how perfectly lovely and amiable, who is the great parent and author of all loveliness? Whatever sweetness and excellency you find in the creatures is but a faint ray of the Creator's perfections, and was reflected from him upon them, to give you an idea of his loveliness. Admire him therefore in it. In all the beauties of nature you may trace the beauties of Jesus Christ the God of nature, who is the first cause, from whom they all flow, and who is the last end, into whom they will be all finally resolved.

But I need not enlarge upon this point. God has certainly every perfection in himself. He is altogether lovely. But in what respects does he appear so to sinners? While they are under guilt, and sensible of their danger, they have no reason to love God: for being transgressors of his holy law, condemned by its just sentence, which conscience owns to be just, subject to present death and to eternal misery, how can they see any thing lovely in that God who may get glory to all his attributes by their destruction? In this view they must see every thing that can make God terrible, but nothing to render him lovely. Until they know, that he will be reconciled unto them, and forgive them all their sins, they can have no reason to love him. The gospel alone can set forth to them the loveliness of God; which it does by revealing unto us an incarnate God, God and man united in one Christ, who is altogether lovely in the eyes of his redeemed people, as I purposed in the *third* place to consider.

All our hopes of heaven are founded upon this truth, that God was in Christ reconciling the world unto himself: for if the man Jesus was not united to the most blessed God, our religion is the grossest idolatry, and christians are of all men most miserable. But the scripture has left no room to doubt of the union of the two natures in one Christ. *The word was God, and the word was made flesh,* says St. *John,* so that God the word was made flesh and incarnate. *God was manifest in the flesh,* says the beloved apostle *Paul.* And the reason was, he was manifested for our salvation. And it was expedient, that the Saviour should be both God and man, because he was to obey and to suffer for us as man, and to merit by his obedience and sufferings

sufferings as God, and thereby to be a complete Saviour. Accordingly he who thought it no robbery to be equal with God the Father, took upon him the form of a servant, and was made man. He obeyed, he suffered, he became obedient unto death, even the death of the cross; and when all the ends for which he obeyed, suffered, and died, were answered, then it was not possible that he should be holden any longer of death. Justice releafed him on the third day from the prison of the grave, and he rose again triumphant from the dead; whereby believers had full evidence given them, that all the demands of the law were satisfied, that Christ's sufferings had made a full atonement for what they should have suffered, that he had taken out the sting of death, and had opened unto them the gate of everlasting life: for as he stood in their place, as their great representative, all his victories are theirs, and by faith they know and are affured of their interest in them. And through him, who loved them and gave himself for them, they shall be saved from sin, and satan, from suffering and death, from hell and everlasting torments. And they shall not only be saved through him from these their spiritual enemies, but

but they shall also receive joys unspeakable and full of glory, a happiness greater than tongue can utter or heart conceive, a crown incorruptible and undefiled, and that fadeth not away: for they shall be made kings and priests under God and the Father, and they shall reign for ever and ever in fulness of joy both in body and in soul; and all this shall be the free gift of God through Jesus Christ our Lord.

Thus the Lord Jesus under the character of the incarnate God is altogether lovely. He has every grace and perfection, that can render him amiable in the eyes of believers: for to them that believe he is precious. And he has every thing that can recommend him to the esteem of awakened and convinced sinners. He is just such a Saviour as they want. He has every thing to give, that they stand in need of. The God-man has an inexhaustible fountain of grace, which always stands open for the relief of weary and heavy-laden sinners, who come unto him seeking rest unto their souls. He calls unto them with his sweet voice — Ho every one that thirsteth, come ye to the waters of comfort and salvation. Lo, here is pardon and peace,
righteousness

righteousness and holiness. All the graces that can make you lovely in the sight of God the Father — all the glories that can make you happy with him in eternity, are in my power to give. I purchased them for such sinners as you are, and I give them freely — Ask and ye shall have, seek and ye shall find. And what should hinder them from answering him? Yea, they will answer. This is the very language of their hearts — Lord Jesus, help our unbelief. We are convinced, that all the graces of time and all the glories of eternity are thy free gift, and we bless and praise thy holy name for putting it into our hearts to seek for the enjoyment of those graces and glories. All the loveliness of this lower world, all the loveliness of heaven itself is thine, centers in thy person as in the incarnate God, and flows from thee as God made man, on purpose to make us filthy and abominable sinners lovely in the sight of thy heavenly Father. Oh that we may see clearly our interest in thee, and may know the incarnate God to be our Lord and our Saviour, and then our faith will behold thee altogether lovely, and shall admire no loveliness, unless it bear thy fair image,

image, and what leads us through its beauties to adore and praise thine.

And if Christ appear in this amiable light to those, who are only seeking, and desiring to experience his love and mercy, what thoughts must believers entertain of him? How must they value him? Certainly, he is with them altogether lovely. And have they not good reason to think him so? For what loveliness is their in heaven or earth but his? Is there not in his manhood every grace that can adorn the human nature? Is there not in his Godhead every infinite and eternal perfection? And do not these perfections flow through the manhood of the incarnate God to render vile and polluted sinners altogether amiable and lovely? God and man were united in one Christ in order to save them from their sins, and he puts them into perfect possession of many of the benefits of his salvation, as pledges and earnests of his bestowing more: for he now awakens them and raises them from the death of sin to newness of life, he pardons their past rebellions, sends his good Spirit into their hearts to shed abroad in them the comforts of his pardoning love, to fill them with joy and

and peace in believing, to enable them to mortify the body of fin, and to put on the new man which after the image of God is created in righteoufnefs and true holinefs. All this is prefent falvation, the happinefs of which is great beyond defcription. Oh come then my brethren, tafte, and fee what the Lord Jefus has to give. Whatever your ftate and circumftances are, he can make you completely happy: for he has engaged that all things adverfe as well as profperous fhall work together for good, for prefent and eternal good, to them that love him. And when you can love him, becaufe he firft loved you, then you will find that he is able to do exceeding abundantly for you, above all that you can either afk or think.

Upon this fhort view of our Lord's character it appears that he is altogether lovely. He certainly has, as man, as God, and as the incarnate God, every perfection of heaven and earth. All that is amiable in itfelf, or ought to appear amiable to us, meets in him, and therefore if we love what is amiable in itfelf, or what is good to us, we ought to give the firft place in our hearts to the Lord Jefus. And does he then reign in them? Is he the
fole

sole Lord of your affections? Do you, my brethren, love him in sincerity, with a pure uncorrupt love, and with all your hearts, and with all your minds, and with all your strength? Is his kingdom set up within you, and is it your delight to do the will of your Lord, and of your God? Grace be with all them, who thus love the Lord Jesus. But alas! their number is but small: for melancholy it is to see, how little the generality of men called christians love him, who is altogether lovely. The transient perishing objects of sense, the vanities, the follies of life, appear more lovely and have more of their hearts than that God whose servants and worshippers they profess themselves to be. Nay the abominable deformity, and horrid ugliness of sin seem to them more lovely. What can be the reason, that men professing christianity should be so inconsistent, and should make such a wrong judgment in so plain a case? Surely they must lay under some great delusion: for not to love him whom they call their God, and who is altogether lovely, is both a disgrace to their boasted reason, and is also acting against their own present and eternal interest. Sin is the cause of this monstrous delusion. It blinds

the

the sinners understanding, that he does not see his want of a Saviour, and consequently he cannot judge of the Saviour's worth. While he thinks himself whole, he sees no occasion for the physician. But so soon as conscience awakes, and he is made sensible of his guilt, and feels his misery, then he will desire the assistance of the great physician of souls, and will begin to value him. The more deeply he is convinced of sin, the more earnestly will he apply to the Lord Jesus who is able to save him from his sins. And as he partakes of the graces and blessings of salvation, the Saviour will grow more and more lovely in his eyes. And when conscience ceases to accuse, when the law no longer condemns, but he finds joy and peace in believing, then the Saviour will be altogether lovely. The believer will form higher ideas of him, than he can find words to express: yea, he knows, that his ideas of him cannot rise up to the greatness of his Lord's merits. As man he is far exalted above the children of men, as God he is over all blessed for ever, and as God incarnate, he is the continual joy of the believer's heart, and the sweet subject of his praise here in time, and the song of the glorified spirits in heaven will be upon the riches of his grace,
and

and they will never be able to exhauſt the ſubject, or to ſearch it to the bottom, becauſe the riches of Chriſt are unſearchable and infinite, and eternal.

Here then we are come to the root of the matter. Jeſus is altogether lovely; but why do not all men who profeſs to worſhip him think him ſo? Becauſe they do not find their want of him. They are under no concern about their ſins, and have no deſire to know the pardon of them, and therefore they ſee no reaſon to eſteem the Saviour of ſinners. They are ignorant of their own wants, and therefore they know not his worth; but baſely, wickedly prefer the worthleſs things of this life to the Lord and giver of life and glory. Is not this the ſad ſtate of the generality of our people? And does not this evidently prove, that they are chriſtians only in name? They have none of the ſpirit and power of their religion, but in their lives diſhonour that holy name by which they are called.

My brethren, are any of you in this ſtate? Look up to God and beg of him to ſhew you the true ſtate of your ſouls, that you may ſee how much you are concerned in
what

what has been said. Are you indeed lovers of the Lord Jesus? is he in your eyes altogether lovely? When the objects of sense flatter, and present themselves to your choice in the most alluring dress, then do you see your beloved Saviour the chief among ten thousand? Can you give up ten thousand of them for him? For him can you reject with disdain all that the world calls great and honourable, looking upon Jesus to be all and in all? If you are not in this state, be assured that your hearts are not right with God: and if you neither see the perfect loveliness of Jesus Christ, nor desire to see it, then you are still under the power of sin, deluded and blinded by it, and if God does not open your eyes to see the delusion, death will soon open them to your everlasting confusion. But if God has convinced you of sin, and you find your want of a Saviour, wait upon him, and he will give you many happy proofs of his perfect loveliness. You will experience his love in pardoning your sins, in justifying you from the guilt of them, in making you the children of God, and in fitting you for his heavenly kingdom. Daily as you find your interest more clearly in his redeeming love, you will partake more and more of his

exceeding

exceeding great and precious promises, whereby your love to him will increase, and you will find him more lovely. Faith will open to you the riches of his love, and shew you how precious he is: *for to them that believe he is precious*—He is precious indeed to the believer: and he is not precious to all men, because they do not see their want of him, nor know what his free grace can do for them: for he has invited all weary and heavy-laden sinners to come and experience how happy he can make them. Whatever their wants may be, he is willing and able to supply them. If ye be but sensible of them, ask, my brethren, and he will relieve you. Be ye ever so black in yourselves, he can make you comely. Be your sins ever so many, ever so heinous, in his righteousness you may be presented before God the Father without spot of sin unto salvation. Have you thought ever so meanly of him, his good Spirit can give you reason to entertain more noble sentiments. Your ingratitude, your very blasphemies against him may be pardoned, and much ingratitude, and many blasphemies are no bar to his free grace. This is the sweetest part of our Lord's character, and ought above all to endear him unto those who

see

see their want of his help. Let them come ever so late, ever so guilty, the arms of his mercy are open to receive them. If you see nothing but sin in yourselves, yet go to him. His blood cleanseth from all sin. Implore his mercy, and see whether he will cast you out. Be not discouraged by looking into yourselves; you may be deformed enough, but remember that he is altogether lovely; and by faith you will know his loveliness is yours. He will wash you clean from every stain of sin in his most precious blood, and will present you before his Father in spotless purity. Be ye ever so defiled with uncleanness, have lust, drunkenness, or gluttony polluted the body, and the love of the world, and of the things of the world still more polluted the soul, yet the fountain is open. Go, wash, and be clean. Sins deep as scarlet shall be as white as snow, sins like crimson shall be as wool. They that are washed in the Redeemer's blood, stand before God's tribunal, as white as snow, without spot of sin unto salvation.

My dearly-beloved brethren, can ye believe these things, do ye assent to them, and yet are you not determined to apply to Jesus Christ

Chrift for his graces and bleffings? He invites you to come to him, and will you not come? Be ye ever fo unworthy, he will make you worthy. Be ye ever fo abominable in the fight of God, he will make you lovely. All your wants he is able and willing to fupply. Why then do you chufe to live without his graces and bleffings? They may be had freely. Afk, and ye fhall have. Only exprefs your wants. Beg a fupply from his bounty, and he, that has done all for you, will do all in you. Go then with your wants whatever they be, to the throne of grace, and the incarnate God will fupply them. He is more ready to give than you can be to afk. His heart is large and open. It is the fame tender heart which once bled to death for finners, it cannot want love. And he is now on the throne of glory; he cannot want power. Apply to this loving God and Saviour of finners, and he will convince you of *your* wants, and of *his* worth. He will beftow upon you out of his fulnefs grace for grace, until you acknowledge with thankful hearts that the Lord Jefus is altogether lovely.

My

My christian brethren, you can bear me witness, that I have spoken but a small part of the Redeemer's praise: for you believe him to be true and very man, and true and very God, united in one Christ, and you know by sure scripture-marks and evidences, that the one Christ is your Saviour; whereby you are interested in all that he did and suffered as man, and merited as God, and has now as king-mediator to bestow. Being thus enabled to say, " My beloved is mine, " and I am his," you are convinced that *your* beloved is above all blessing and praise. You cannot reach the greatness of his merits. The poverty of language, the weakness of the human understanding, the coldness of your affections are so many hindrances to your speaking of your God and Saviour as he deserves. And when you try to get over these obstacles, and have some hopes of success, yet then you find the corruptible body so presseth down the soul, and the earthly tabernacle so weigheth down the mind, that praise dies away upon your lips. But you hope there is a time at hand, when your praises will be more perfect. When you shall be freed from all the frailties of this mortal

mortal life, you will then be better able to difcover, and more conftantly difpofed to celebrate, the lovelinefs of your redeeming God. But even then you will not be equal to the fubject. Your praifes will be but finite, and the adorable Redeemer is infinite. There is no proportion between them. No more than between time and eternity; and fuppofe you continue your praifes to eternity, yet your happinefs, your crowns of glory and palms of victory, your ftanding confirmed in blifs are the free gift of God in Jefus Chrift our Lord. And how then can you worthily extol the riches of his free grace? How can you pay the debt, that you owe to free grace? When you have praifed him for millions of years, Jefus is ftill as lovely, your praife as much due, your joy in offering it as great, as when you began. There is ftill the fame majefty in the brightnefs of that glory, which fhines in the face of Jefus Chrift. He is the light of the heavenly *Jerufalem*, and light you know is fweet, yea a pleafant thing it is to behold the fun. Oh how fweet, how pleafant then muft it be to fee the fun of righteoufnefs fhining in his glory? Surely he will then appear altogether lovely. Bleffed are the eyes that fhall then

fee

see the king in his beauty, and happy, for ever happy, are they who shall then praise him; but even then the highest strain of praise of angels and men united will not come up to the greatness of his merit. He will be more lovely than all the tongues of all the heavenly host will be able to express. And if the glorified spirits thus fail,

O thou incarnate God, whose glory the heaven and heaven of heavens cannot contain, pardon the low opinion we entertain of thine infinite excellencies, pardon the imperfect manner in which we have been speaking and thinking of thee. Thou knowest, Lord, that we desire to know thee more, and to praise thee better. Arise then, O thou bright and morning-star, and shine into our hearts, dispelling the darkness of our understandings, and taking away the depravity of our wills and affections, that we may see thy loveliness, and our interest in it; and enable us daily to love thee more and more, until we behold thee face to face, and then we shall know, that our Saviour and our God is altogether lovely. Oh thou adorable Jesus, admit us all to this blessed vision and fruition of thy Godhead. May all this congregation be in the happy number of thy redeemed people, who are to praife and admire thine infinite lovelinefs for ever and ever. So be it to the honour and glory of Father, Son, and Holy Spirit, three perfons in one Divine Effence, to whom be equal praife and worfhip in heaven and earth, in time and in eternity. *Amen* and *Amen*.

SERMON VIII.

Chap. v. Ver. 16.

This is my beloved, and this is my friend.

IN the last discourse I endeavoured to recommend to you some of the loveliness of Jesus Christ. It was only some part of his loveliness: for we know it at present but in part. It is infinite, and surpasseth all understanding. The most enlightened mind cannot fully comprehend it, no not in heaven. We shall not be able in eternity to discover all the perfections of our incarnate God, and how then can we think or speak worthily of them at present? We must fall below the majesty of the subject, but that is no reason we should not treat of it. It is our duty and interest to think and to speak of our blessed Saviour in the most sublime ideas, and in the highest expressions, because we cannot exceed the greatness of his merits. He is above all blessing and praise; and

and so you will believe, when you know him to be *your* Saviour. When the spirit of wisdom and revelation enlightens the eyes of your understanding, then you will behold some of Christ's loveliness; and when you are enabled to say with true faith—*This is my beloved, and this is my friend*—then his loveliness will appear to you with a new grace and excellency, because you will then see your interest in it.

This is the particular view, in which I shall consider our Lord's loveliness at present. The believer knows him to be his beloved, and the perfections of Christ appear with a peculiar beauty through this endearing relation, because he can truly say—He that has these perfections is my beloved, and my friend, he has them for me, I have a sure interest in them in time and in eternity. My brethren, do the perfections of Christ appear to you in this light? Can you take up the words of the text, and repeat them from your own experience? I fear there are not many of us who can: for the generality of men, called Christians, choose other beloveds, and other friends, than Jesus Christ. Many of them have no love for him,

him, or if he has any place at all, yet he has not the first place in their hearts and affections, no not even in theirs, to whom he has been most bountiful. Where his favours have been great, there one might expect great returns of love, but we find no such thing in fact. Not many worldly-wise and learned, not many rich and noble repay his favours with thankfulness. Though Christ be altogether lovely, and ought to appear so to them, yet few of them love him. What can be the reason, that men of genius, whom Christ has blessed with great gifts and talents, should make him no suitable returns of gratitude? And that men who profess themselves to be his worshippers should have no love for their God? The true cause is, they are in love with sin, and it blinds them. Christ is all beauty, but they have no eyes to see it; no not even a desire to see it, until they begin to find the exceeding sinfulness of sin. When conscience is uneasy about the pardon of their sins, and they feel their want of a Saviour, then they will begin to desire his salvation, and God will hear their desires, and will open their eyes to see a precious Christ, and will give them faith to believe in him to the saving of the soul.

Faith

Faith makes Chrift appear precious: for it is the proper office of faith to enable us to behold Chrift's excellencies, and it is the proper work of that faith, which worketh by love, to let us know our intereft in them, by which every excellency appears to us more lovely. And the text defcribes this office, and alfo this work of faith. The believer firft declares that Chrift is altogether lovely, and then that he knew Chrift's lovelinefs was his. *This is my beloved, and this is my friend.*—He is my beloved on whom my heart and mine affections are entirely placed, becaufe he firft loved *me*, and gave himfelf for *me*. He has fhed abroad his love in my heart, and I know that my beloved is mine, and I am his.—He is mine—my friend—who has my welfare at heart, and who will deny me nothing, that can make me happy in time and in eternity. May the Spirit of the Lord Jefus open all your underftandings to fee, and all your hearts to receive thefe comfortable truths, while I am difcourfing upon the words, and opening the fweet doctrine contained in them, by fhewing

Firft, What Chrift has done to make himfelf the beloved and the friend of every believer.

Secondly,

Secondly, The believers knowledge of his interest in it, before he could say, this is my beloved, and this is my friend.

Thirdly, From whence arose the certainty of his knowledge.

Fourthly, The happiness he had in knowing certainly, that Christ was his beloved and his friend. And then I will apply the whole as God shall enable me to your consciences.

And *First*, I am to shew what Christ has done to make himself the beloved, and the friend of every believer.

If men followed the common instincts of nature, and had no bias to turn them from their own interest, he would be the beloved friend of the whole world: for is there a more natural or stronger instinct, than the love of pleasure and the hatred of pain? We are subject to innumerable pains both in body and soul, in this world and in the next, and we have very few enjoyments, that can be called real pleasures. Sin was the cause of all our misery. It robbed us of our pleasures, and brought upon us our pains. All was good,

good, until sin entered into the world; but when it entered, all evil entered with it, the evil of pain to torment our bodies and bring them down to the grave of death, the evil of guilt to torment our consciences, and the evil of punishment beyond the grave, where soul and body were to receive the wages of sin. From these evils the Lord Jesus came into the world to save his people. And he took our nature that in it he might bear our griefs and carry our sorrows. The holy law of God accused us of transgression, and he came to answer the demands of the law, which he did by paying it a full and perfect obedience, and this obedience, being the act of a divine and infinite person, had therefore a divine and infinite merit to atone and satisfy for sin. For transgressing the holy law of God we were liable to suffer the threatened pains and penalties, Christ in our nature suffered them for us, taking our sins upon him, and bearing the griefs and sorrows and death due to them; for the scripture declares, that he was made sin for us who knew no sin, and that he bare our sins in his own body upon the tree, and that by his stripes we are healed. And he demonstrated that these sufferings were infinitely meritorious, when

he

he rose from the dead for our justification. And thus by his active and passive obedience he wrought out an all-perfect righteousness for us, and when the Holy Spirit enables us to lay hold of it by the hand of faith, then being thus applied and made ours, we are not only freed from condemnation and redeemed from the curse of the broken law, and from all the pains and penalties due to the breach of it, but do also receive a right and title to the present graces, and to the eternal blessings purchased for us by the obedience and sufferings of our most blessed Lord and Saviour Jesus Christ.

Now let us examine how the forementioned instinct operates in the present case. We all love pleasure, and hate pain. This is an universal principle in human nature. And here is a Saviour who promises to deliver us from the present and eternal pains to which sin had subjected us, and to give us of his spiritual and heavenly pleasures here in time and in eternity. He is able to fulfil his promise, for he is the Almighty God. He is willing: for as his power is, so is his love; both are alike infinite. And indeed he is daily fulfilling his promise unto all true

believers,

believers. But are all men seeking freedom from pain and enjoyment of pleasure at his hands? Do their desires, their affections move to him, with the same natural instinct with which they would fly from sickness and pursue health? Let matter of fact speak. How are men found to act with respect to Jesus Christ, who has present salvation to give them from sin and its effects in his kingdom of grace, and the pleasures of eternal salvation to bestow in his kingdom of glory? Alas! he is despised and rejected of men; although he became a man of sorrows on purpose to carry our sorrows, and acquainted with grief, that he might bear our griefs, yet they hide as it were their faces from him. The haters of pain choose sin with all its miseries, rather than accept of the great salvation of our God, and the lovers of pleasure prefer the empty perishing joys of sense to the solid and everlasting joys of his heaven. In what relates to the soul they act against that very instinct, by which they are invariably guided in what relates to the body. What can be the reason, that the same men should act so inconsistently in a case so exactly parallel? Sin is the true cause. Sin has destroyed the use of the intellectual faculties

in

in all spiritual matters, and by cutting off all communion with God who is the fountain of spiritual life, has left the soul in a state of death, even dead in trespasses and sins. The soul of every natural man is represented in scripture to be as dead to all motions of grace, as dead to God and to the things of God, as a lifeless corpse is to the things of this world. Talk to it of its wants, it feels them not. Recommend to it the Redeemer's sweet graces and divine excellencies, it has no desire to find an interest in them: because it feels not its wants of them. To persons in this state Jesus Christ cannot appear lovely. Notwithstanding all that he has done and suffered to endear himself to sinners, yet while they see an engaging form and comeliness in sin, they can see no form or comeliness in the Saviour that they should desire him.

But when one of these persons is awakened from the dead sleep of sin, when his eyes are opened to see himself, when he has a clear view given him of his sinful heart and of his wicked life, and the Spirit of God sets home the conviction of sin upon his conscience, and makes him sensible of his guilt and

and of his danger, then he will find his want of a Saviour, and will fee a peculiar fuitablenefs and fitnefs in Jefus Chrift to fupply all his wants. He has every office, and every qualification that an awakened finner could wifh. He is juft fuch a Saviour as his heart could defire; and when he begins to fee Chrift in this light, then he will begin to appear lovely in his eyes. And when out of the riches of his grace he begins to fupply the finner's wants, then he will become more lovely: for the more any man knows of Chrift, the more he will love him. But when the pardoned finner taftes the fweetnefs of redeeming love, and finds joy and peace fhed abroad in his heart by the Holy Spirit, when he can fay Jefus Chrift loved me and gave himfelf for me, then the beloved Saviour appears altogether lovely, becaufe he fees his intereft in the obedience and fufferings of the God-man. He can take up the words of the text, and fpeak them upon his own experience, which leads me

Secondly, To confider the believers knowledge of his intereft in Chrift, before he could fay, *This is my beloved, and this is my friend.*
Here

Here he applies to himself what Christ had done for sinners, as the ground of his love and friendship to him. He had been made to see his wants. The soul being awakened had found the burden of sin intolerable, and had gone weary and heavy laden to Jesus Christ, and he had given it rest. The soul being convinced of sin, felt the torments of a guilty conscience, which nothing could quiet and comfort, but the atoning blood of the lamb of God; and when this was sprinkled upon the conscience, it felt the sovereign healing virtue: for the blood of Jesus quenched the hell within, and brought down heaven into the soul. The Holy Spirit bore his inward witness, that this was the work of God; and he continued the heavenly joy of his first testimony, by enabling the believer to shew the reality of the inward work by the outward evidence of his life and conversation, by bringing forth the rich and ripe fruits of the Spirit to the glory of God. And thus he had good evidence of his being interested in the obedience and atonement, in the righteousness and sanctifying grace of Jesus Christ, and lived in sure and certain hope of inheriting through him immortality and endless glory.

The sinner must experience these things before he can say of the Redeemer, *This is my beloved and my friend.* He must find in himself these proofs of Christ's love and friendship, which he was to shew to sinners. He had wisdom and pardon, righteousness and holiness, and eternal redemption to give them; but my gratitude and love cannot arise from his having them to give to sinners in general, but to me in particular. I must have reason to call them *mine*, he must enable me to apply and to appropriate them to myself, before I can see his loveliness in giving them; because it is not what he does to others, but what he does to my soul, that makes him *my beloved and my friend.* And hence came the wise remark, which was so often made by our first reformers, " That " an unapplied Christ is no Christ." All that he has done and suffered for sinners must be applied to me, before I can call him *mine.* He is the wisdom and the light of his people, but how can he appear to me altogether lovely in this character, if I am still in ignorance and darkness? How can I love him for being made unto me wisdom, until he has enlightened me with saving truth? He has pardon to give to the greatest sinners,

sinners, but if it be never made out to me, I can have none of the comforts of it; and how then can I love him for being the pardoner of sin, " unless I feel my conscience at " peace with God, through the remission of " my sin," as our church expresses it in the third part of the homily for Rogation Week? He has the robe of perfect righteousness to bestow, but if I know nothing of my being cloathed with it, the law will still condemn and my conscience will be full of guilt and horror; and how then is it possible for me to love him for being the righteousness of the saints, if I never find joy and peace in believing that his righteousness is imputed unto me for my justification? He is the believers holiness and sanctification, but how is he mine, while I find myself enslaved to sin, and kept under its dominion? How can I love Christ for being the sanctification of his people, while I am under the absolute power of sin? Christ is also made unto the believer redemption, but if I know nothing of my having received redemption through his blood, even the forgiveness of sins, how can I lift lift up my head with joy, when the almighty Judge is coming in the clouds, as knowing that my redemption then draweth nigh? in

like

like manner all Chrift's gifts and graces are matter of joy to the pardoned finner, fo far as he receives them, and knows by faith his intereft in them; without this knowledge, of what benefit can they be, or what comfort can they adminifter to any perfon? For if you be fick, and have an excellent remedy that would cure you; yet it can do you no fervice, unlefs you take it. Suppofe you are perifhing of hunger and thirft, fetting meat and drink before you will not fave your life, unlefs you ufe them. If you are naked and like to be frozen to death, will thofe cloaths warm you and fave your life, which you never put on? So Chrift is the medicine of the fin-fick foul, but if Chrift's virtue be not applied to heal, if the medicine be not taken, how can it work a cure? So he is the bread of life, but unlefs he be taken and verily and indeed received as fpiritual food, how can he fupport the life of God in the foul of man? So Chrift is the cloathing of his people, but how can he be their cloathing, if they never put him on? How can they appear before God in fpotlefs purity, if they have never put on Chrift Jefus the Lord? Surely then there is great judgment in that wife faying, which our reformers

had

had so often in their mouths, "An unapplied Christ is no Christ"—he is no Christ to that sinner to whom he is not applied, and therefore he is not his beloved nor his friend.

From hence appears the manner and kind of knowledge on which the believer grounded the words of the text. He was able to apply to himself all that Christ had done and suffered for sinners. He knew it experimentally. He had the comforts of it in his own heart, and seeing clearly his interest in Christ, he therefore saw him altogether lovely.

But perhaps some one may ask, Can I apply the merits of Christ's obedience and sufferings so clearly and safely to myself, that I may be sure I am not deluded? This is a very important enquiry, which I shall pursue, under my third head, wherein I was to consider what certainty I can have of Christ's being my beloved and my friend. The scripture promises us full and complete evidence, and it is the office of faith to enable us to rest upon it. Our certainty arises from our faith, and from what faith shews us of our own particular intereſt in God's promiſes. The word of promiſe and the Holy Spirit applying the word muſt go together: for the word is but a dead letter, unleſs the Holy Spirit animate and quicken it, by working faith in the heart to apply it ſavingly. Faith is a divine grace given us by the Spirit of God on purpoſe to convince us of our intereſt in Jeſus Chriſt, and to enable us to apply the promiſes to ourſelves: for it is expreſsly ſaid to be *the gift of God* — and to be wrought in us by *the operation of God* — By his almighty operation he works in my heart a clear conviction of my being accepted at the bar of juſtice, as juſt and righteous, through the righteouſneſs of Jeſus Chriſt. When the Holy Spirit has given the believer this clear conviction, then he has divine authority both from the word of truth and the ſpirit of power, to call the Saviour his beloved and his friend. The Holy Spirit muſt enable him to do this: *for no man can ſay that Jeſus is the Lord but by the Holy Ghoſt*; and therefore without the Holy Ghoſt how can any man ſay, that Jeſus is *my* Lord? Indeed he will be ſo far from ſaying it, that he will queſtion whether it can be ſaid with certainty,

tainty. The natural man who has not the divine grace of faith is always reasoning against it, and concludes with himself, that it is altogether presumption. He cannot see, how it works full assurance in the mind. And how should he? As he is a stranger to the thing, how should he judge of the nature of the evidence which it gives? He is a more improper judge, than a blind man is of colours: for until he receive faith from God as his gift, and by the operation of God as the work of his Spirit, he can form no idea of the nature of the certainty, which it produces in the mind. The scripture teaches him, that faith is the evidence of things not seen, even such evidence as gives them a present substance and reality; so that the whole man, and every faculty of soul and body rest upon the certainty of them with full assurance, and direct every word and work towards the attainment of them: but the natural man receiveth not these things. How the eye of faith should be open to see what is to the natural man invisible, seems to him a great mystery. And so it will be, until God open his eyes. He only can do it: yea, he only can convince him that he is now blind. Oh that the enlightening Spirit

may

may open the eyes of every perfon here prefent who has no certainty of his intereft in Chrift, that he may not only be convinced fuch a thing is to be attained, but may alfo be led to feek, until he find, all the comforts of it, which comforts I propofed in the *fourth* place to confider.

The comforts which I here fpeak of are realities — promifed in God's infallible word — beftowed by his Spirit — and received by faith. They no more depend upon fancy and imagination, than the objects do which we fee with our eyes and handle with our hands. The foul has as true a perception of them, as the bodily fenfes can have of any folid fubftance. And you may as well fay, we are deluded at our common meals when we are eating or drinking, or when we are hearing a fine piece of mufic, as fuppofe righteoufnefs, and peace, and joy in the Holy Ghoft to be a delufion. Thank God the believer knows, and is happy in knowing the reality of thofe things. When he can fay with the apoftle, Jeus Chrift loved *me*, and gave himfelf for *me* — And with the faithful in the text — He is *my* beloved, and he is *my* friend, then he has the prefent
poffeffion

possession of the graces and blessings purchased by the Redeemer's obedience and sufferings, and the eternal possession is secured to him under the seal of two infallible witnesses, *viz.* the word and the Spirit of God. The comforts, which he enjoys in this state, can no more be described than the joys of heaven. He has a love which passeth knowledge, a peace which surpasseth all understanding, a joy which is unspeakable and full of glory. In one word—the Comforter is his. The eternal Spirit, whose name, whose office, whose glory it is to be the comforter of God's people, is his. He is the applier of all comfort, and he dwells in the heart to apply it; what comfort then can be wanting? He is the sinner's comforter: for he comes to give him faith, and to assure him of his pardon and acceptance. He is the believer's comforter in all times and states, strengthening and establishing him, shedding abroad in his heart that love, which makes prosperity safe, and adversity sweet, and which renders even the way of the commandments delightful. And this divine comforter is the dearest pledge of our Lord's love: " for he shall take of mine, " says the blessed Jesus, and shall shew it unto
" you,"

"you," even to all his disciples and followers to the end of the world. He shall take of my graces and blessings, and shall shew them unto you, shall manifest them and your interest in them to your hearts. I will send him for this purpose. In this one gift, he sent you all: because he sent you that Spirit who lets you know your interest in all: knowing this you are happy, yea happier than tongue of men or angels can describe. Your loftiest descriptions fall short of the happiness, which the Lord Jesus gives by his Spirit in the present life: and they who taste of it find that he is altogether lovely, and are assured that he is their *beloved* and their *friend*. May the God of all mercy and consolation assure every one of you of your interest in the Redeemer's friendship, that you may receive many happy proofs of it in time, and in eternity.

And now let us look into ourselves, and apply what has been said to our own hearts. You have heard what the Lord Jesus did and suffered to make himself the beloved and the friend of all believers, and what knowledge he gives them of their interest in his obedience and sufferings, nay what certainty they have

have by faith of their interest in him, from whence flows a continual source of pure and spiritual comfort. Since these things are so, the matter is now brought to a point, and that is; can you, my brethren, take up the words of the text, and upon the clear evidence of your own experience declare, Jesus Christ is my beloved and my friend — He is mine, and I am his — His good Spirit bears testimony of it in my heart — The word of God bears testimony of it in my life: for I am become a new creature, and live a new life in Christ Jesus. If you can say this with truth, then you are happy. But if you cannot, you want the true foundation of gospel comfort which is laid in Christ Jesus, and in the evidence I have of my interest in him.

But perhaps some of you may think, that there is no knowing for certain, and others may think it presumption for a man to declare, that he knows so much of the state of his soul, as to be certain that Christ is his beloved and his friend. Hear what the scripture says: " Jesus Christ," says the blessed apostle *Paul*, " loved me, and gave himself " for me." Certainly this was not presumption in *Paul*, nor yet in the beloved *John*, when

when he said — "The Son of God hath
"given us an understanding, that we may
"know him that is true, and we are in him
"that is true, even in his Son Jesus Christ."
He did not think it any presumption to declare that he was in Christ, rooted and built up in him.

But these apostles some will say were inspired: they knew this by inspiration, but is it the common privilege of all believers to know it? It is. Every true believer knows that Christ Jesus is his Saviour and his God. Faith manifests it to him; and faith is wrought in him by the operation of the Holy Spirit for this very purpose. So says our church in the third part of the *Homily of Salvation*, "The true faith is a sure trust
"and confidence in God that by the merits
"of Christ my sins be forgiven, and I am
"reconciled to the favour of God and am
"partaker of the kingdom of heaven by
"Christ." And in the third part of the *Homily for Rogation Week* our church says,
"that a man may feel his conscience at peace
"with God through remission of his sin." So say the living members of our church. They can use her words without presumption, and
declare,

declare, that they have a sure trust and confidence in God that by the merits of Christ their sins are forgiven, and they are reconciled to the favour of God, and are partakers of the kingdom of heaven by Christ, and that they feel their conscience at peace with God through remission of their sin. What can you object to these authorities? The liturgy will not suffer any member of our church to make the least objection: for in the prayer after the communion service we are taught, " That God does *assure* them, " who have duly received these holy mys- " teries, of his favour and goodness towards " them; nay more assures them that they " are very members incorporate into the " mystical body of his Son, and also assures " them, that they are heirs through the hope " of his everlasting kingdom." Here our church plainly teaches, that a believer may know Christ to be his beloved and his friend: for he may have assurance of God's favour and goodness towards him, the assurance of his being united to Christ, and incorporated into his mystical body, and the assurance of his being an heir of Christ's everlasting kingdom. The warmest contenders for the assurance of faith could not have expressed

their

their opinion in stronger terms, than our church uses in this prayer. And now, my brethren of the church of *England*, what do you think of these authorities? Are they not clear and dicisive? And will you not be determined by them? Here you have the word of God, and the Spirit of God, and the people of God with one voice declaring, that a man not only may know, but that it is the very office and work of saving faith to let him know, and to *assure* him of, the favour and goodness of God towards him, and that he is a member of Christ, and an heir of glory. Do not then, my brethren, deny a fact so well attested. Your denial of it will only prove your want of true saving faith. And it is a very strong proof to others, would to God you saw your want of it yourselves. At present you dispute gainst the certainty which faith gives, because you have not received it, nor have any desire for it. Is not this the case? This shews your want of that faith, which is the operation of God. When faith is the work of his grace, it brings absolute certainty. According to the apostle it gives substance to the things hoped for, and evidence to the things not seen. If you have not this kind of faith,

don't

don't dispute against it, lest you should be found disputing against God. Rather beg of God to give it you. Ask him, if it be the privilege of believers to know Jesus Christ to be your beloved and your friend, to give you this knowledge. Ask it for the sake of your present and eternal peace. If you desire a calm serene conscience free from the guilt of sin, and saved from the power and dominion of it, beg you may know your interest in the Lord Jesus: for until you know it, you cannot live upon the promises nor enjoy the comforts of the gospel. You cannot live upon the promises but by faith, by that faith which makes the things hoped for substantially present, and realizes the things not seen, and thus enjoys the comforts of the gospel. But as you have not this faith you live without Christ in the world, and if you should come to die without any hope in him, Oh think what your condition would then be. All your sins would stand unatoned against you. Conscience would accuse. The broken law would condemn you. Justice must give you your due; and what? but the wages of sin, even eternal destruction of soul and body. Are not these very interesting and alarming considerations? I pray

pray God to give them their proper weight and influence upon your minds. May he convince you of your want of faith, and stir you up to seek it as the free gift, and as the work and operation of the almighty Spirit. Thus seek and you shall find. Continue seeking with humility in the ways of the ordinances, and you will be brought to the knowledge of a loving Saviour, who will give you many reasons to call him *your* beloved and *your* friend.

If then you are convinced of sin, and see your guilt and your danger, what should hinder you from accepting the blessings of Christ's love? Is it the sense of your unworthiness? He is the Saviour of the unworthy. Are you afraid he will not receive you, because you are great sinners? He came to save the greatest. But you have been high and long in rebellion against him. Then you stand in greater need of pardon. Make more haste to obtain it, and apply more earnestly for it. But you find so much weakness and backwardness in yourself that you are at a loss how to take one step: this is another motive for applying to him. Read for your encouragement that sweet scripture,

"The

"The son of man is come to seek and to save that which was lost." Go then to him such as you are, go as poor lost sinners, for such he came to seek and to save. He is the beloved Saviour and friend of sinners. His love to them brought him down from heaven—carried him through a blaspheming persecuting world — nailed him to the cross, and laid him in the grave. Can he want love for sinners, who did so much, who bled to death for them? What can he with-hold from them, who is now their advocate, pleading their cause, and interceding for them at the bar of justice? Oh sinner, consider what a blessing it is to have an advocate with the Father, Jesus Christ the righteous, who is willing and able to supply all thy wants. Make them known to him. Open thy heart before him, and acknowledge thy great and numerous sins. Confess them, and they will be no bar to his love and friendship. He will do honour to his free grace by making thee out a full pardon. The Holy Spirit will be sent to bear his testimony of it in thy heart, he will give thee love and joy in believing, he will cloath thee with the perfect righteousness of Jesus Christ, he will enrich thy justified soul with his sanctifying graces,

graces, mortifying sin in thee, and making thee alive to God; and he will make thee happy in having the most high God and Saviour for *thy* beloved and *thy* friend here in time and in eternity.

All this and more than this the Lord Jesus will do for every unpardoned sinner, who will apply to him. No tongue can relate the greatness and number of the graces and blessings which he has to give to sinners. Faith has a present taste of them, and hope now enjoys them, and though imperfectly, yet no description can come up to what the believer feels; and who then is able to describe, how great they will be when faith and hope shall cease, and the soul shall be filled with the love of God. Oh what happiness, what a heaven will it be to see our Saviour in the brightness of divine glory! To behold him face to face — and then to be able to say of *him*, whom all the host of heaven worship, of the eternal and almighty God whom all the redeemed adore — this is my beloved and this is my friend; that will be joy unspeakable. Oh how lovely, how altogether lovely will this blessed God then appear in the eyes of sinners, when his love and friendship shall have brought them safe to the enjoyment of his eternal glory! How will they then admire and praise the wonders of his redeeming love! What subject of joy, and gratitude, and thanks will their consideration of his free grace afford them, which raised them from the lowest state of wretchedness to the highest happiness of his heaven. Certainly their blessedness surpasseth all understanding. No tongue can utter or heart conceive, how great it is. And yet, sinner, all this may be thine. The Lord Jesus promises it freely. Come then and accept of it. Unless thou thinkest thy sins can make thee happier than God can, return to them no more. Now close in with the invitation that is made thee. Take Jesus for thy God. Go this day, this hour to the throne of his grace. Commit thyself into his hands, sinful as thou art, and he will send his good Spirit into thy heart, to give thee present comforts of salvation, and to prepare thee for the eternal salvation of thy Lord and thy God.

And now what wait we for, O thou most blessed God and most loving Saviour, but that we may all experience the truth of this scripture. Write it Lord Jesus in all our hearts.

hearts. Send us away with warm impreſſions of it upon our minds. Oh that every ſoul here preſent had reaſon to ſay, Yea, he is altogether lovely—Whatever is lovely in heaven and earth meets in the incarnate God, and this incarnate God is my beloved and this is my friend. May the grace of the Eternal Three, of Father, Son, and Holy Spirit, manifeſt to your ſouls the perfect lovelineſs of Jeſus Chriſt, and keep him *your* beloved and *your* friend in time, until you ſee him face to face in his eternal glory. *Amen* and *Amen.*

SERMON IX.

Chap. vi. Ver. 1.

Whither is thy beloved gone, O thou fairest among women, whither is thy beloved turned aside, that we may seek him with thee.

IN the beginning of the 5th chapter we find the believer fallen into a spiritual slumber. After much sweet communion with Christ, and long walking in the light of his countenance, he grew negligent. While the bridegroom tarried he slumbered and slept. He left off stirring up the gift of God that was in him, and ceased to be watchful and to strengthen the things which remain. And thus he forgot the rule laid down for the conduct of believers—" Let us not " sleep, as others do, but let us watch and " be sober."

Christ is represented as coming to the soul sleeping in this security, but it was not a total, universal

universal sleep, like the dead sleep of sin: for he found the heart awake, and capable of distinguishing it to be his voice, that knocked at the door of the heart for admittance and said, " Open to me, my sister, " my love, my dove, my undefiled, for I " have been waiting till my head is filled " with dew, and my locks with the drops " of the night." The soul, willing to enjoy its indolent slumber, excuses itself from rising to let him in. Upon which he withdrew himself, and hid his face. He took away the sensible feeling of his comforts, but at the same time left something in the heart, which made it sensible of its past unkindness, and put it upon endeavouring earnestly to recover its former communion and sweet fellowship with Christ. The soul is restless until they be recovered,—goes out to seek for Christ, but cannot find him—calls, but he gives no answer—meets with reproach and persecution in the search, and yet gives it not over—turns to the daughters of *Jerusalem*, the outward members of the church, and charges them if they found her beloved to tell him, that she was sick of love; she had enjoyed the sweetness of his presence, and now so distinctly discerned his absence, as to be sick and in pain for the return of his love. Instead of answering directly, they enquire, " What is thy beloved more than " another beloved, O thou fairest among " women, what is thy beloved more than " another beloved, that thou so chargest us." This question gave occasion to the believer to describe his beloved. He draws a character of Christ, and paints his excellencies under the most sublime images nature could afford; but finds all too mean to express Christ's worth, and his value for it. He therefore sums it up in these words—" Yea he is " altogether lovely — This is my beloved " and this is my friend, O daughters of " *Jerusalem*."—Although he has withdrawn himself, yet still he is altogether lovely in my eyes: for I know that I am interested in him, and this gives a new grace to his every excellency. Still he is my beloved and I am his, still he is my friend and I am his. Although he has for a time hid his face from me, yet I believe that e'er long I shall again walk in the light of his countenance. This enlivened description of Christ fired the daughters of *Jerusalem*. They now saw there was something more in this beloved, than in another beloved. And they had

had good desires stirred up in their hearts, earnest and fervent desires, to share in his love, and to partake of his graces and blessings: for thus they now reply, in a very different temper to what they shewed before—" Whither is thy beloved gone, O thou " fairest among women, whither is thy be- " loved turned aside, that we may seek him " with thee." May the Holy Spirit by his gracious influence dispose every one of us to seek, as they did, until we find, an interest in the blessed Jesus. And to this end may he accompany with his grace and blessing what shall now be offered,

First, Concerning the character of the persons who speak the words of the text.

Secondly, Concerning the subject-matter of their speech. And

Thirdly, Concerning the use we are to make of it.

And *First*, The persons who speak in the text are called " the daughters of *Jerusalem*." *Jerusalem* is the church. The scripture applies the word, both to the congregation of
the

the faithful here below, and also to the heavenly *Jerusalem* that is above. The daughters of the church are its members, who were bred and educated in it. They lived in her communion, and partook of her ordinances. And yet they seem to have had no experience of that sweet and spiritual union which the believer enjoyed with his beloved Saviour: for they enquire what he saw in Christ more than in any other beloved, and being made acquainted with his graces and excellencies, then they desire to seek him along with the believer. These circumstances plainly prove that they were not intimately and vitally united to Christ by faith. They were not joined to him as the head of the mystical body, nor as his living members were they drawing nourishment and strength from him for the support and carrying on of their spiritual life. They were not as living branches grafted into the true vine, and bearing much fruit by their union with him; but they contented themselves with living within the pale of the visible church, and thought themselves safe and happy in church membership. They were the children of *Abraham*, admitted into the covenant on the eighth day, lived among
God's

God's chosen people, who had the law and the promises, and they were strict in the observance of the instituted rites and ceremonies. Easy and secure in this state, none of them enquired—All these have I kept, what lack I yet? One thing thou lackest—spiritual communion with Christ, without which church privileges and outward ordinances do not answer the end of their appointment. It is the Spirit that quickeneth, the flesh profiteth nothing. The flesh, the outward service, profiteth nothing, unless the quickening Spirit go along with it. And the quickening Spirit has not gone along with it, until he has begun to draw the soul to Christ, and to unite it to him by faith.

If we look among the members of our church, we shall find too many followers of these daughters of *Jerusalem*. We have some, who because they live in the communion of a sound apostolic church, therefore think themselves safe, while their lives give open scandal and offence to all good men. Their opinion about good mother church is very much like the opinion of the *Papists*, who think the living in the church can save them, although they live in their sins. And we have

have others, who make the greateſt boaſt of their love to our church, and ſpeak of her in the higheſt terms, who are only outward members of her communion. They will contend with all their might for the purity of her rites and ceremonies, and will draw their ſwords to defend the divine inſtitution of epiſcopacy, and to cut off from all communion with Chriſt thoſe vile ſchiſmatics who will not live in the communion of the church of *England;* while they have not a word to ſay for the neceſſity of being united to the head of the catholic church, and of being joined to him by living faith. Nay, perhaps, when they hear, that unleſs the Holy Spirit be the bond on Chriſt's part uniting him to the believer, and faith on his part uniting him to Chriſt, it will be of very little conſequence in what outward communion a man lives: when they hear this, it is too hard a ſaying, they cannot bear it. They think, that a ſound church with a good liturgy, ſcripture articles and homilies, and a regular diſcipline, are the main things. Doubtleſs they are good things. God forbid our church ſhould be without them, and God forbid any member of our church ſhould reſt in them: for in this communion,

excellent

excellent as it is, a man believing it to be excellent may yet live without the grace of Chrift, and perifh from glory for ever. The church is not a Saviour. We *Proteftants* have one Saviour, even Chrift Jefus our Lord. The *Papifts* indeed make a Saviour of the church, and a far greater Saviour than Chrift: for the holy mother church can fave a man who dies in his fins unrepented of, which Chrift has no where in fcripture promifed to do. And our high churchmen in the heat of their party zeal fpeak and act in the very fpirit of *Popery*. By laying fo much ftrefs, nay laying all the ftrefs, as fome of them do, upon outward communion, they omit the weightier matter of inward communion with the head of the church, without which, of whatever reformed church or *Proteftant* congregation a man be a member, he is no member of the true church of Chrift. He has not the fpirit of Chrift uniting him to the head of the myftical body, and without the fpirit of Chrift he is none of his. Reft not then, I befeech you my brethren, in outward memberfhip to this or that communion. Don't place your religion in externals. You may live in the beft communion upon earth, and fuch indeed I take the church

of

of *England* to be, and yet you may be out of Chrift's kingdom. Outward things of themfelves will not avail: for the kingdom of God does not confift in meat and drink, or in any thing external, but in righteoufnefs, and peace, and joy in the Holy Ghoft. His kingdom is a fpiritual thing. It is formed within us, in the heart. There Chrift muft rule and govern. Seek then to have his kingdom fet up within you by an inward work of his grace. Beg of God to fhew you your want of it, and when it fhall pleafe him to convince you, that no outward things can avail, not even his own inftitutions, unlefs his quickening Spirit be in them, then he will bring you into a proper frame and temper of mind to join with the daughters of *Jerufalem* in the text in feeking the knowledge of your intereft in Chrift, which is the *fecond* particular to be confidered.

The believer had defcribed the excellencies and perfections of his beloved Jefus, and had fpoken feelingly of his own intereft in them. The defcription ftirred up the daughters of *Jerufalem*, who wondered at firft what he faw in his Jefus to be fo enamoured with him, to defire that they might have the
fame

same happy experience. And they, who could enquire before what there was in *him*, more than in another beloved, now ask, " Whither is thy beloved gone, O thou " fairest among women?" Christ had before called her the fairest among women. She had no beauty in herself—defiled and deformed with natural and actual guilt, she was cast out to the loathing of her person. He that is of purer eyes than to behold the least iniquity, could not see any thing in her but ugliness and sinful deformity; and yet the love of the Lord Jesus has cleansed her from every spot and stain of sin. In the 16th chapter of *Ezekiel* we have a sweet description of his free grace and love. " When " I passed by thee," says he, " and saw thee, " polluted in thine own blood, I said unto " thee when thou wast in thy blood, Live; " yea I said unto thee when thou wast in " thy blood, Live."—And after describing the several steps which he took to raise her up, to ornament her, and to ennoble her, he adds—" Thy renown went forth among " the heathen for thy beauty: for it was " perfect through my comeliness, which I " had put upon thee, saith the Lord God." He cloathed her with the unspotted robe of

his

his own righteousness, and made her perfect through his comeliness which he put upon her. All our comeliness now consists in what Christ puts upon us, and in what he works in us. While man was innocent he wanted no cloathing; but when he lost the image of God, then shame and sin made cloathing necessary. The sinful body is forced to go to the creatures to borrow a covering from them, and the soul has no covering but what comes from the head of the church. The moon has no light but what she receives from the sun. The spouse of Christ shines in the beams of her husband. Covered and ornamented with his righteousness, and enriched with the graces of his Spirit, she is the fairest among women, fair in the sight of an infinitely holy God, in the eye of the perfect law she appears to be without spot or wrinkle or any such thing, holy and without blemish. In this amiable light she now appears to the daughters of *Jerusalem*. They see and acknowledge her perfect beauty, and earnestly desire to partake of her Lord's love. Whither, say they, is thy beloved, whose love was able to cloath thee with this immaculate robe of righteousness, and whose spirit has enriched thee with so many divine graces, whither is he gone? They knew he had withdrawn himself from the believer, but it's plain from this question, that they did not think Christ had quite forsaken him; they supposed he still knew Christ, and was able to inform them whither he was gone. The words immediately following the text shew, that he was acquainted where Christ then vouchsafed his presence, though he had hid his face from him—" My beloved," says he, " is gone down into " his garden."—He is still in the garden of his church. There he was to be found. He was still present by his Spirit in the ordinances, and in them he was determined to wait until he found his beloved. Christ had taken away the light of his countenance, not only to chastise his former sleepy security, and to make him more earnest in seeking his Lord, and to make him more thankful when he should find him, but also to render him the means as it here proved, of stirring up others to seek for a clear knowledge of Christ, and the experience of his love—" Whither is thy beloved gone," say they, " whither is thy beloved turned aside?" —not wholly departed, but only turned aside, tell us, " that we may seek him with thee."

How

How wonderfully does grace appear to work by the growth of these good desires in the daughters of *Jerusalem!* And how ready should we be to speak a word for Christ, since such may be the happy effects? How industrious ought we to be to seek occasions, how careful to neglect none? As we know not which word is to prosper, either this or that, let us take every opportunity of saying something for Christ. Let us inform men what he is, and what we know of him, and who can tell but a very imperfect, yet well-meant description may receive a blessing. Have we not great encouragement in the morning to sow our seed, and in the evening not to with-hold our hand, from the success mentioned in the text? When the daughters of *Jerusalem* heard the believer enlarge upon the excellencies of Christ, and set forth his own share and interest in them, and saw that no discouragements could cool the ardor of his love, they were hereby stirred up; these were the means under God of putting them upon desiring a nearer and more close acquaintance with Christ. They knew him before by profession, but now they wanted the possession of him. They wanted to know Christ to be theirs. At first they saw no form nor comeliness in him, that they should desire him. But now the desires of their hearts are after him. They see their want of him, they are convinced of his all-sufficiency to supply their wants, they believe he is able, and they hope he is willing, they neither doubt of his power or of his love to save, and therefore they resolve to seek him, untill they have experienced the truth of the character which they had heard of him, and can call him *their* beloved and *their* friend.

Considering the words in this light, they hold out to us one plain lesson. When the daughters of *Jerusalem* heard of the beauties and excellencies of God the Saviour it wrought upon their hearts, and kindled fervent and earnest desires to know their interest in him. Still God works in the same manner. When Christ is set forth in his divine graces, and attributes, and offices, the Holy Spirit thereby stirs up desires in the hearts of sinners to seek Christ and his salvation, and he also excites holy affections in believers to follow Christ more closely. Has he, my brethren, wrought thus in any of your hearts? How have you been affected with these discourses

courses upon the loveliness and perfections of Jesus Christ? Have they made any good impression upon you? Have you had stronger desires after Christ, and have you seen him more lovely than you ever did before? These effects ought to have followed: for his "name is as ointment poured forth," the preaching of his name is like opening a box of the richest perfume. It diffuses its fragrancy all around, so that the house is filled with the grateful odour of the ointment. Did you perceive none of it poured forth, none of this unction from the holy one descending upon you this day? Did you find no sweet favour of grace working in your hearts, while I was attempting to draw a short character of the loveliness of Jesus? Did he appear to you altogether lovely, as man, as God, as God-man united in one Saviour, and was it the prayer of your soul, that you might find him your beloved and your friend! If the Holy Spirit accompanied the word, these effects have followed; if they have, give the glory to God, and be thankful; and if they have not, Oh that he may now enable me to speak a word to your consciences under my *third* and *last* head, which was to make a proper use and application of what has been said.

The believer, though under spiritual desertion, could see nothing worth seeking after, but his beloved Saviour. He seeks him, though he cannot find—calls, though he has no answer—continues seeking and calling, though he meets with disgrace and persecution. The pleasing remembrance of their love would not suffer him to rest until it was renewed. His love grew with seeking. Opposition made it burn the brighter. He went on, nothing discouraged, until he found the daughters of *Jerusalem*, and made them acquainted with his case. They ask, what he found in this Jesus, that he was so distrest at his withdrawing himself from him? this gave him occasion to draw the character of his beloved, which he does in a very enlivened description, setting forth in the most beautiful colours, what he was in himself, and what he was to him, the perfect loveliness of Christ, and his interest in it. Upon this the daughters of *Jerusalem* take fire. They become also in love with Christ, and desire to share in those perfections, the account of which had touched their hearts and inflamed their affections.

Now

Now if the Spirit of God be moving in your hearts, this is, my brethren, the cafe with you. You are convinced of your own fpiritual wants, and of Chrift's being an allfufficient and a loving Saviour, and while I have been defcribing him, you have fent up many a wifh to heaven, praying him to reveal himfelf to you, and to manifeft his love to your foul. This is always the confequence of preaching Chrift Jefus the Lord, when God effectually works with the word preached. When the Holy Spirit accompanies it with his divine grace, it is then the power of God unto falvation. But

If this has not been the effect, if you have had no defires awakened in your minds after Chrift, confider I befeech you, what a ftate of guilt and danger you are in. Jefus Chrift has all the excellencies of heaven and earth, every thing that ought to gain your efteem in his human nature, every thing that can demand your love in his divine nature, and as God-man united in one Saviour he has every grace and every bleffing to give, that can make you happy in time and in eternity. And yet though he has every thing valuable, that can win the underftanding, though he has

has every thing defireable, that can gain the will, though he has every thing lovely, that can influence the heart and the affections, you can hear of him without any emotion. You fee no form nor comelinefs in him that you fhould defire him. Without an intereft in him you muft be miferable for ever. He alone can fave you from the juft punifhment due to your fins, and yet your hopes and fears, your own intereft, your love of pleafure and hatred of pain, cannot prevail with you to love and efteem the God of our falvation. What is the reafon of this? Why are all the faculties of the foul thus ftrongly biaffed againft their own intereft? Propofe to them any fenfual pleafure, they eagerly defire, and ardently purfue it, and with the fame propenfity they fly from fenfual pain. But in matters relating to the foul they act directly contrary. Jefus Chrift being the Saviour of the world has every fpiritual pleafure to give, and yet they neither eagerly defire, nor ardently purfue it. Without an intereft in him body and foul will be in everlafting pain, and yet they do not fly to him, that they may avoid it. Whence is it that men act thus abfurdly, thus unnaturally? The fcripture gives this

reafon.

reafon. Sin has corrupted all the faculties of foul and body, and has got dominion over them. It has blinded the underftanding, which is dark, yea darknefs itfelf the apoftle fays, not only without the actual knowledge of God and of the things of God, but alfo without the potential knowledge of them: " for the natural man perceiveth not the " things of the Spirit of God." From whence we learn his actual want of knowledge in the things of God. But left fome fhould afcribe this to his neglect of them, or to his not being acquainted with metaphyfics or moral reafoning, the apoftle adds, " neither can he " know them," let him ftudy them ever fo much; from hence we learn his want of power to know them, and this is the reafon, " becaufe they are fpiritually difcerned."— An evident proof, that the faculties of the natural man are as much under the power of fin as a dead corpfe is under the power of death. In all fpiritual matters he is like a dead man, without any fpiritual difcernment. He cannot turn his mind to think, his will to defire, or his affections to love them. Sin has abfolute dominion over him, and forces him to ferve it with all the powers of foul and body, even to their own deftruction.

tion. In this state, dreadful as it is, you are at present. If the desires of your heart be not after Christ, if you do not at this time wish from your souls, that you may have an interest in the loveliness and excellencies of Christ, and may know him to be your Saviour and your God, then be assured that you are still under the power of sin. It has entirely blinded you, and I should be an enemy to my blessed master, and an enemy to your happiness, if I did not speak to you freely and openly, and warn you of your danger. Out of love to your souls I cannot be silent, and whether you will hear or whether you will forbear, I must deliver my own soul.

I suppose, my brethren, you profess yourselves christians, and you believe that Jesus Christ is a perfect and complete Saviour, and you believe farther, that you shall some time or other stand in need of his salvation; but you have no desire to experience it at present. You do not want present salvation from sin. You cannot but wish to be freed from the guilt and punishment of it, but then you have no wishes to be freed from its dominion; is it not evident therefore that it still

has

has dominion over you: and being so, you are children of God's wrath, under the curses of his holy law, sentenced by it and condemned to everlasting torments, death will soon come, and inflict the curses of the law upon you, even the most terrible and dreadful of them. How awful and striking are these words! Who but a man dead in sin could stand out against the force of them? " If any man love not the Lord Jesus Christ " let him be anathema maranatha." You are here put under the heaviest and bitterest of divine curses, not only if you hate or oppose Jesus Christ, but also if you do not love him. Oh consider then and weigh this scripture carefully, if you have not some love for the Lord Jesus, and are not seeking to love him more. I leave it upon your minds, and may God write it upon all your hearts, that you may fly from this anathema maranatha to the arms of that loving Saviour, who alone can deliver you from it. Flee then from sin. Flee then from satan. Flee from all the enemies of your souls to this loving God, who is almighty to save. And to those who are flying to him for salvation, and whose hearts have been stirred up to seek him along with these daughters of *Jerusalem*, I make my *second* practical remark.

My

My brethren, you have great reason to be thankful for these first motions of grace. God has begun to draw you to himself — follow and run after him. Seek him, while he may be found. And for your encouragement remember how many sweet promises God has made in scripture to them that seek him. " Those that seek me early, says wis- " dom, shall find me." *Prov.* viii. 17. Christ, who was made unto us wisdom, here declares that he will be found of them that seek him. And again he says, " Seek and " ye shall find; for every one that seeketh " findeth. These are the words of the God of truth, and they shall stand fast for ever and ever. His almighty power will against all opposition fulfil his promises. And his faithful people find them fulfilled. They have the comfortable experience of them. One of his people, a man after his own heart has declared, " Thou Lord hast never failed " them that seek thee."— No, never — at no time has he disappointed them. If they sought happiness in him, they infallibly found it. And this is the experience of all God's people. They can take up the prophet's words, and with one voice declare, " Thou " Lord hast never failed them that seek thee." Here is comfort for them that seek the Lord Jesus.

Jesus. How happy would worldly men think themselves, if they were upon this footing, if they were sure of finding what they seek? Let them not rise up in judgment against you, my brethren, and condemn you for not seeking what you could not but have found, if you had sought aright: Christ is to be found in his own ordinances. He is to be met with, not in the wilderness of the world, but in the inclosed garden of the church. Thither he still comes down, and manifests himself to them that seek him. In the assemblies of his people he will be made known by animating and quickening the word, and by rendering it effectual to awaken sinners from the dead sleep of sin, to encourage seekers to go on until they find, and to build up and strengthen them that have found. He will prove himself to be the God who heareth prayer, by hearing and answering their petitions for themselves, and their supplications for all men. He will make himself known to them, by breaking of bread, and by feeding and strengthening their souls with his body and blood at his own table. He still comes down with his gracious presence into these ordinances, and animates and enlivens them. We are his witnesses: for we find his good Spirit in them.

Oh

Oh continue then seeking, and continue in the ways of his own appointing, and when it will be most for his glory, and for your comfort and salvation, you have his word of promise *you shall find*. And sooner shall heaven and earth pass away, than the least tittle of any of his promises shall fail: " Seek and ye shall find." And to them who have found, I have a word of exhortation in the *third* and *last* place.

My christian brethren, since you know Christ to be altogether lovely, and to be *your* beloved and *your* friend, pray daily for more and more of his love. Beseech the Holy Spirit to shed it abroad abundantly in your hearts, that you may honour him more in your lives, and praise him more with your lips. How meanly soever men may think of him, be not ye ashamed to own what he has done for your souls. Publish his praises. Proclaim to all about you, what a loving Saviour you have found. If you after what you have experienced, were silent, surely the very stones will cry out. Speak out then, and tell of his matchless excellencies, and infinite perfections, and try to stir up others to seek. Press them to leave sin, and to come to him, for nothing but sin can

can keep them from him. Perfuade them to leave the poor unfatisfying joys of fin, and to feek his heavenly pleafures. Among your accquaintance and friends, in your family, in all companies, fpeak a word for your dear Saviour. He fometimes bleffes a well-meant fpeech, if it be neither learned, nor elegant. But if it fhould not be a bleffing to others, yet it will certainly be one to yourfelf: for he hath promifed — them that honour me, I will honour.

The fcope and defign of what I have faid was to perfuade you all to feek the knowledge of your intereft in Chrift's love, as the only means of making you happy. Knowing your intereft in him is the ground of your love: for if you had no knowledge or experience of his love, how could you love him becaufe he firft loved you. Your love is only the reflex act of his love. And you muft know that he loves you, before you can be truly happy, and you muft be happy in him, before you can have any motive to fing his praifes from your heart. It is the bleffed employment of the faithful upon earth, and of the glorified faints in heaven, to give honour and bleffing and praife to the Lamb that was flain, and hath redeemed them

them unto God by his blood. Can you, my brethren, join your hearts and voices with theirs? Are you able to praise the Lord for his goodness, and to declare the wonders that he hath done for your soul — to be telling of his salvation from day to day, every day, and all the day. If you have not reason enough to be always giving of thanks, you may be assured you are not a real member of the church of Christ. If you were, you would find the truth of this scripture — " Blessed are they that dwell in thy house, " they will be always praising thee." This is the sweet employment of those who dwell in the house of God, in the church here below. It is meet, right, and their bounden duty, that they should at all times and in all places give thanks unto thee O Lord, holy Father, almighty, everlasting God. It is their duty, and they reckon it their privilege; and sorry they are when they either find themselves interrupted by the necessary affairs of this life, or through coldness of their affections are indisposed for the delightful exercise of thanksgiving. But thanks be to God who will soon deliver us from both these hinderances. E'er long we shall join the glorified spirits who are now standing round the throne, singing the praises of God

and

and the Lamb. This is their conſtant and happy employment. And his infinite adorable perfections will find them freſh matter of praiſe to all eternity. Suppoſe any of you were to go out of the world in love with ſin, and void of the love of Chriſt, you could not join them, nor would it be any pleaſure to you to hear them aſcribe bleſſing, and honour, and glory, and power to him that ſitteth on the throne, and to the Lamb, for ever and ever. This is the felicity of an innumerable company of angels, and of the ſpirits of juſt men made perfect: but it could be none to you, becauſe your heart was not fitted for it. If you believe this, and if God's word be true you cannot deny it, then aſk yourſelves, Would you chooſe to die unfit for the joys of heaven? Surely you would not. Why then do you live unfit for them? If ever you reliſh them, you muſt begin to taſte their ſweetneſs here. In this life the praiſes of Chriſt muſt be your delight, if they ever be in the next. Weigh theſe motives, and give them the attention which they deſerve. Conſider them under the influence of the Holy Spirit. Pray for his grace. And may he diſpoſe you to ſeek the knowledge of your intereſt in Chriſt, and enable you to wait until his love be shed abroad in your hearts; and then you will have reason to rejoice in your redeeming God in time and in eternity. And that this may be your happy experience, let us pray for it. May he who sitteth upon the throne hear and answer.

Look down with mercy, O thou almighty and loving Saviour, upon this whole congregation. All hearts are open, all desires known, and no secrets are hid from thee. O cleanse the thoughts of our hearts by the inspiration of thy Holy Spirit, and enable every one of us to form a right judgment of what we have heard. Stir up, we pray thee, thy power, and come among us, and with great might convince those persons of their guilt and of their danger, who are seeking happiness in the world, and put it into their hearts to seek it in thee. Teach them, blessed Lord, that there is no true happiness to be found in a world, which lieth in sin. Let them experience the delusion of all worldly joys, that they may seek for those joys which thine almighty love has to bestow. And to those, whom thou hast given grace to seek, give more grace. Confirm and strengthen the good desires of those who are waiting for
thy

thy falvation. Keep them by thy power, until thou fave them from their fins. And fave us all, O thou Lord God omnipotent, fave us from the power of fin. Deliver us more and more from its dominion. May all the Lord's people ferve him out of a pure heart, and with love unfeigned; and may they go on rejoicing to do or to fuffer his will, until he, who got himfelf glory by them upon earth, fhall be glorified in them in heaven, by beftowing upon them an exceeding and eternal weight of glory. And when he cometh thus to be glorified in his faints, and we know not how near the day of his coming may be— Oh may it be your happinefs and mine then to be found at his right hand, to hear the almighty Judge pronounce us bleffed, and to enter into the joy of our Lord, there to praife Father, Son, and Holy Spirit, three felf-exiftent perfons in one Jehovah, to whom be honour and glory, dominion and power, thankfgiving and worfhip now, and for ever and ever. *Amen.*

SERMON X.

Chap. viii. Ver. 5.

Who is this that cometh up from the wilderness, leaning upon her beloved.

WE have in these words a beautiful representation of our Lord's love to his people. In whatever light we consider him he is amiable and altogether lovely. He is not only great and good, but has also every thing that is great and good united in him, whereby he is able and willing to save poor sinners unto the uttermost. They can want nothing but what he has to give. And happy for them, his heart is large and open. He is not straitned in his bowels. He gave proof of it in the days of his flesh, when he never refused any person that came to ask his help. And no weary heavy-laden sinner, who comes to him for his promised rest, has ever since been cast out. He is free to pardon and to cleanse them from all their sins, and to bring them
into

into a ſtate of acceptance with God ; and then he is able to keep them through faith unto ſalvation. This is a ſweet part of our Lord's character — he is able to keep them from falling. They are weak in themſelves, but he is ſtrong, and by faith his ſtrength becomes theirs. They are engaged in a dangerous warfare, and have many powerful enemies, but the captain of their ſalvation has conquered them, and has promiſed to make them alſo more than conquerors. They have many troubles from within and from without, but he knows how to make them all work together for their good. He is able to carry them ſafely and ſweetly through all dangers. In this amiable light he is conſidered in the text. He is here drawn with every grace, which can recommend and endear him to the affections of his people : for he does not leave them to find their way through the wilderneſs, nor to overcome the difficulties of their paſſage through it, nor to get ſubſiſtence in it, but he conducts and carries them ſafe through all, while they lean upon him for ſtrength : for he is here ſupporting the church, while ſhe is journeying through the wilderneſs of this world to the promiſed land of everlaſting reſt. And the church is every believing foul—thou makeſt part of it whoever thou art, who canſt place thy truſt and confidence upon Jeſus Chriſt. Thou feeſt the perfect beauty of this image, and knoweſt what it means for the church to come from the wilderneſs leaning upon her beloved. O that the Eternal Spirit may teach you all what it means. He can open your eyes to ſee the ſenſe of it, and can open your hearts to feel its ſweetneſs. The experience of it will make it ſweet indeed, and God grant you may now enperience it, and may be able to lean upon Jeſus Chriſt for his grace and bleſſing on what you hear, while I ſhall

Firſt, Take the words in the ſame order they lie in the text, and endeavour to give the ſenſe of them. And then

Secondly, While I ſhall apply the doctrine to your ſpiritual benefit and improvement.

The perſon celebrated in this divine ſong is Jeſus Chriſt, and his graces and infinite perfections are here deſcribed under the moſt ſublime and affecting images. His love to the church, that is, to every believing ſoul, is

the

the grand design of this highly-finished painting. The manner of the composition is in the way of dialogue. The principal speakers are Christ and the church, and twice or thrice the daughters of *Jerusalem*, or some standers by are introduced, in order to ask leading questions, which would give occasion to the answerer to open the subject more fully. These persons are, I suppose, the speakers in the text, and make the enquiry—*Who is this that cometh up from the wilderness leaning on her beloved?* Who is this? The answer is, it is the church, of whose love to Christ this divine poem treats. And the church is neither the *Jewish* nor the *Gentile*, neither the *Protestant* nor the *Papist*, neither the *Calvinist* nor the *Lutheran*: for the multitude in all outward churches is the same. A man in his natural unregenerate state is just the same, whether he be a *Papist* or a *Protestant*; but the few in these outward churches who live and walk in the spirit and power of Christ, they are *the church*. Every believing soul is a part of it; for of numbers of them the church is composed. Whoever is united by faith to Jesus Christ, who is the head of the church, he is a living member of it. All the rest are dead formal professors,

of whom God knows we have too many. The generality of our people content themselves with a foolish notion of their belonging to the church of *England*, and of their being members of the established church, although they seldom see the inside of a church. They live in ignorance of her doctrines, and in disobedience to her discipline. But may not the persons, who frequent her services and constantly attend upon the outward ordinances, think themselves mighty good churchmen? They may, if they be united by saving faith to the head of the church; but without this union a parcel of loose stones thrown together in a heap would make just such a church as they are. Whereas the spiritual building of which Christ is the chief corner-stone is fitly joined together and compacted in every part; and the cement or bond of union which keeps all the lively stones of this spiritual houshold in their proper place and station is faith, as the apostle has taught us, *Heb.* iii. 6. " Christ is a son
" over his own house, whose house we are,
" if we hold fast the confidence of faith,
" and the rejoicing of hope firm unto the
" end." If you attend ever so much upon the outward ordinances, yet if you have not
this

this confidence of faith, and this rejoicing of hope, you make no part of the church of Chrift. You want the proper cement of this fpiritual building. You are but loofe ftones, and therefore neither united to it, nor any part of it. You come to prayers—you attend twice a day on *Sundays*—you go once a month to the facrament—All this is very well, and you may go thus far, nay much farther, and yet be no member of Chrift's myftical body. For thefe outward fervices profit nothing, unlefs the heart be rightly difpofed: and the heart is then rightly difpofed, when we go to thefe fervices in faith, hoping to meet God in them, and to receive fuch fupplies of grace from him as we ftand in need of. But when men ufe the ordinances in hopes of making themfelves good, and of attaining fome felf-righteoufnefs, then they abufe them, and the ftricteft attenders upon the ordinances with this view are the worft churchmen, becaufe they moft effectually cut themfelves off from all union with the head of the church. By going about to eftablifh their own righteoufnefs, they entirely deprive themfelves of that righteoufnefs of Jefus Chrift, without which no man fhall fee the Lord. If the felf-righteous could

could be made to confider this, they would not reft in forms and ordinances, which are only the beggarly elements of religion when refted in, but would feek the grace of God, which is the life and fpirit of the ordinances, and then as they are his appointed means, he would certainly be found in them. And whoever finds him in them, and thereby receives continual fupplies of grace for the advancement of his fpiritual life, he is a member of the true church of Chrift.

Our reformers have given us an excellent defcription of the church in their 19th article. "The vifible church of Chrift is a congre-
"gation of faithful men, in the which the
"pure word of God is preached, and the
"facraments be duly adminiftered according
"to Chrift's ordinance." Here they allow none to be members, no not even of the vifible church, unlefs they be faithful men: faith uniting them to Jefus Chrift is that which makes them good churchmen, as it will evidently appear from a farther confideration of this fcripture: for the condition of the church is the next particular—" She
"is coming up from the wildernefs," from the wafte howling wildernefs of this world,

and

and travelling on towards the promised land of everlasting rest.

When man was first created he was placed in a paradise of delight, where God had provided every thing necessary for the support both of soul and body. But when he transgressed the just and holy law of God he was driven out of paradise, and turned into the wide barren world, where his body was forced to labour for the bread that perisheth, and to earn it by the sweat of his brow, and his soul was banished from God and from all sweet communion with him, which had made paradise so much like heaven, and the remembrance of its sweetness would make the pleasantest spot upon the earth appear like a desolate wilderness. As God is the life, and his presence is the happiness, of the soul, what must it be without God? More uncomfortable surely, than the body would be in the most dismal howling desert: and we are all by nature in this state. The world is indeed a place of banishment to every son of fallen *Adam*. What will you call it but a wilderness, where not a morsel of bread grows without human labour and cultivation? And is not this a just picture of the

the state of the soul, which has no divine or saving knowledge of itself, and can receive none from any of the arts and sciences? This barren earth cannot produce one single ray of heavenly truth. It must all come down from above, as manna did upon the *Israelites* in the wilderness, otherwise our souls will perish for lack of knowlegde, as their bodies would have perished for want of bread. And since this is our condition, how shall we obtain deliverance? We are here in bondage. Sin has chained us down in this wilderness. Satan watches us and tempts us to love our chains. The vain world smiles upon us, and would make us believe, that we are still in paradise: and God knows there are too many poor silly creatures who take this world for their only paradise. They are so dotingly fond of it, that nothing can break the enchantment. Though pains and miseries come one upon the back of another, like wave after wave, yet still they cannot entertain one hard thought of this dear world. They love it with all their hearts, and with all their souls, notwithstanding the briars and thorns, which tear and scratch their flesh, and the disappointments and vexation they daily meet with.

with. This fatal delusion is the worst part of their case, because to be in such a wilderness is a great calamity, but to be in love with it is a greater. It is a great misfortune to be sick, but to be in love with sickness, is worse than the distemper, and much harder to be cured. And how then can the soul recover her liberty? She is enslaved and chained down to this wilderness, and her enemies have her absolutely in their power. She cannot stir one step in her own might. Indeed she would not desire to stir. She loves her bondage. And since she has neither the will nor the power, how can she escape out of this wilderness? God be praised, there is a way open, and this is through Jesus, who has declared of himself, " I am the way," and all that fly to him escape from the miseries of this wilderness, and are coming up from it, though not in their own strength. The first desire to leave it was from Jesus Christ; he enabled the soul to seek deliverance, and then gave her strength to break loose from the chains wherewith she was bound, and in his might she is now travelling on. He has given her a prospect of a better country, and for it she has left off seeking happiness in the wilderness. The
honours,

honours, riches and pleasures there to be found have lost their former value. She has turned her back upon them, and has set out upon her journey heavenwards. And see, all the way she is coming up from the wilderness she

"Leans upon her beloved." He supports every step. This is the chief part of the beautiful image in the text. We here see the work of faith painted before our eyes in the most beautiful colours. There could not be a finer picture of the believer's reliance upon Christ for grace to support every step, and for strength to carry him on in the christian life, than to draw the church leaning upon her beloved. To lean and rest the body upon any thing is the perfect representation of faith leaning and resting itself upon Christ. An able expositor upon the passage has these words — " She is leaning on her
" beloved; that is, as they, who are weak,
" make use of a staff in climbing of a strait
" and steep ground, or ease themselves by
" leaning upon one that is strong, and espe-
" cially one whom they love for helping
" them in their way: so the believer is said
" to come up from the wilderness, ' leaning
" on her beloved,' because she being weak
" in

" in herself and unfit for such a difficult
" journey, by faith rests on Christ, for help-
" ing her in the way, whereby she is sus-
" tained, and carried through in the duties
" of an holy walk, and the difficulties in her
" way, till she come through the wilderness
" unto the land of rest."

Every step she takes, spiritually by faith and love, she cleaves to and relies upon Christ. There is a sufficiency, and efficacy in Christ to save to the uttermost, to begin and to carry on, and to perfect the whole work of salvation: he is the wisdom, righteousness, sanctification, and redemption of believers; and therefore they would not only by faith be united to him, and lean upon him for the pardon of their sins by his righteousness, but they would also by faith depend upon him for their sanctification, for their dying to sin, and being alive unto God. And thus by the exercise of faith they fulfil the commandment—" Trust in the Lord with all
" thine heart, and lean not to thine own
" understanding." If they overcome the world the victory is from trusting in the Lord by faith, from the power of Christ apprehended and applied by faith. If sin be dying in them, it is by the efficacy of his

death

death apprehended and applied by faith. If they be alive unto God, " it is not I," says *Paul*, " but Chrift liveth in me." It is by exercifing faith on Chrift, that I receive ftrength to get forward in the way of duty, and to make a progrefs in holinefs. I derive continual fupport from him, and the more I can depend and lean upon him by faith, the fafter I go, and the farther I advance in the way: for leaning on him, and coming up are joined together in the text. If you gain any ground it muft be by leaning upon the beloved Jefus for his fupport and ftrength: for he is "the beloved" here fpoken of. The beloved Son of the Father, in whom he declared he was well pleafed, and he is become the beloved of the believing foul, which is now awakened by his Spirit, and ftirred up by his power to leave this barren wildernefs, and to feek a better country, *i. e.* a heavenly. His love begun the firft defire, and ftill carries it on. His Spirit opened the eyes of faith to fee a better country, and fupports every ftep towards it. And the believer leaning and relying upon his beloved Jefus goes on fweetly and fafely. He beholds infinite excellencies, and daily difcovers new worlds of delight in him; and the fenfe of his own intereft interest in them increases the delight. He can call all these *his own.* And to have a property in them makes them still more valuable. In this divine song he frequently lays a great stress upon this particular, especially in the 5th chapter, where he has been drawing a picture of his Lord, and he puts the finishing stroke to it in these words — " This is *my* beloved—and this is *my* friend." All his excellencies appear with a double grace to me, because I can call them *mine.* This is the happy experience of every faithful soul. May the Holy Spirit bestow it upon you, giving you a view of the Redeemer's excellencies, and convincing you of your interest in them, while I am

Secondly, Applying the doctrine contained in the text to your spiritual benefit and improvement. " Who is this that cometh up " from the wilderness?" It is the believer, whose affections are now raised above all earthly things, and he is coming up from the world leaning every step he takes in the way towards heaven, upon his beloved Jesus. The believer's heavenly mindedness is here represented by his coming up or ascending from the wilderness, wherein he sojourned, in his way to heaven, as the *Israelites* did in the wilderness, while they were on their journey to the *Promised Land*. The believer looks upon the pleasantest and best-cultivated spot of this earth as a mere wilderness, because there is no true comfort or perfect rest for the soul in any of the good things of it. He has left off seeking happiness in the enjoyment of them, being convinced that all worldly joys are empty and unsatisfying, and therefore he has turned his back upon them. He remembers *Lot*'s wife. He would not cast one wishful look after them. He keeps walking on with an unwearied course, because he has an almighty support. He leans upon one who is able to bear up every step, who can strengthen the weak hands, and confirm the feeble knees. Christ is his support in his walk heavenwards. He takes Christ for his sanctification, as well as for his justification. Christ must do all in him, as well as for him. Christ must enable him to do the works proper to a state of acceptance, as well as bring him into it: for the believer knows of no power, whereby he may be enabled to die unto sin, and to live unto God, but his power only, who is almighty to save his people *from* their sins.

This

This is the doctrine. From the first moment our backs are turned upon the world and we begin to leave the wilderness of sin and misery, until we come to the promised land of everlasting rest, we must lean all the way upon Christ. He must be our stay and support. Faith must rely upon him for the success of every thing we undertake, and by this reliance it secures success. The greatest part of our misfortunes and disappointments in our temporal as well as religious affairs come from the ignorance of this doctrine. We know not how to trust all in the hands of our loving Saviour. Worldly prudence will be managing its temporal matters without resigning all to him: and mens pride and self-sufficiency cannot bear to be stript of all merit, and to rely entirely for acceptance upon the merits of another. It is too low and degrading an idea of the dignity of man to suppose him to be in a state of condemnation until Christ justify him, and to be unable to take one step in his christian course unless the spirit of Christ assist and support him. These truths are too mortifying to be generally received, but believers know them to be truths by happy experience. They are assured, that there is no other way to walk contentedly and chearfully homewards, but to lean and reſt all the way upon him, who is both their guide and their ſtrength, who has them and all their concerns in his gracious hands. Although this be the only way to true happineſs, yet it is extremely difficult to convince ſinners of it. Every error leads them away from it, and error is infinite. I will endeavour through God's help to correct ſome of the moſt common errors. And

Firſt, I ſhall ſpeak to thoſe which all careleſs ſinners fall into. Sin cut off all communion with, and reliance upon, God, and whoever lives in his natural unregenerate ſtate cannot rely upon him for any good; the ſinner leans upon ſome worldly enjoyment for happineſs, and the careleſs ſinner is ſecure in this worldly enjoyment. He has no thoughts of ſeeking happineſs in Jeſus Chriſt, and therefore has no deſire to lean with faith upon him. The danger of this is evident, becauſe every man in it is under condemnation and is a child of wrath; and it is wonderful that the devil ſhould be ſo far able to delude ſinners as to make them ſit eaſy under it: for did they but know and feel their condition as it really is, is, sinful and dangerous, they would then acknowledge themselves to be miserable sinners; and were they convinced of their want of salvation, and that there is no Saviour but Jesus Christ, then would they in earnest seek salvation through him, and not as they do, labour to deprive themselves of it with all their might: for they are daily adding to their sin, and to their guilt, and to their misery. When they read, " there is " salvation in none other than Jesus Christ," they are deluded into a false peace, although they are not assured they have salvation in him. When God declares, " that without " holiness no man shall see him," they know they are not holy, and yet they never consider what eternal misery it will be not to see God. Thus these careless sinners being out of a state of salvation, are in danger of perishing every moment. Jesus Christ alone can save them, and yet they prefer sin to him and his eternal salvation. The guilt of this is so monstrous, that men could not fall into it unless they were under a strong delusion. And yet the extreme folly of this conduct is equal to the guilt of it. Men who have no rest nor stay upon Christ cannot be happy in the present world. They are not

upon

upon the foundation, the rock of ages. Their happiness is built upon sand, against which when the rains descend, and the floods come, and the winds blow, it will fall. When the evil day comes these careless sinners have nothing to rest upon. When affliction presses hard upon them, they sink under it. When sickness seizes them, down fall their high spirits, the approach of death is most dreadful, and they sometimes die for fear of dieing. Or if they meet with heavy troubles, they are often so miserable, that life is quite a burden; and if natural conscience should at this time begin to torment them with its horrors, these added to their other distresses would overset them. Having none of the comforts of the gospel to support them under this complicated misery, they often seek relief in self-murder. This is frequently the cause of that dreadful crime, which can never be repented of. And thus these poor miserable cowards murder themselves rather than live in pain, and fly to hell for refuge from the miseries of life. Are not these evident proofs, that there is no solid happiness out of Christ, and that whatever men lean upon for happiness but him, are nothing better than so many broken reeds?

Do

Do we not see these proofs confirmed by daily experience? When God sends any public calamity, the sword or the pestilence, or famine, sinners receive them as judgments, and are terrified, but not reformed. If he arise to shake terribly the earth, their hearts tremble more than the ground does under their feet: they fear lest it should open every moment and swallow them up. If it should, their consciences tell them they cannot escape the pit of destruction. This is the miserable condition of careless sinners, who have no trust and confidence in Jesus Christ. They are an easy prey to every enemy, and they are made miserable by the fears and terrors of their own consciences. And is it not the foolishness of folly to be always tost upon such a tempestuous sea, when you may be saved from all the storms of life? Who would choose to have his peace of mind lie at the mercy of every wind and wave? Is this prudent, is this safe, when he that commandeth the winds and the waves has only to say, " Peace, be still," and there will be a great calm? Thy tempestuous soul will be composed. Thou wilt find a peace of mind that passeth all understanding. Oh unpardoned sinner, hast thou no desire, hast thou no wish

now

now rifing in thy mind for the enjoyment of this peace of God? May he without whom thou canft not fo much as think a good thought, put it into thy heart to feek it. And when thou art once made fenfible of thy fore difeafe, here is thy remedy. Chrift is the infallible phyfician of the foul, and he has a fovereign balm to heal every malady of fin. Does thy confcience accufe and torment? The fprinkling of the blood of Jefus can take out the fenfe of guilt, and give thee joy and peace in believing. Doft thou begin to be weary of thy fins and thy fufferings? Afk Jefus Chrift to take off thy burden. Come to him, who bore all thy fins, and he will eafe thee of thy load, and thou fhalt find peace and reft unto thy foul. He has promifed it to every returning finner, and he is a God of truth. "Caft thy burden upon "the Lord and he will fuftain thee;" this is his promife, and he daily fulfils it. Look among believers and thou wilt fee it literally fulfilled. Thou canft not deny but that being juftified by faith they have peace with God, and are happy in the fenfe of his love to them through Jefus Chrift their Lord; whereby they are fupported and comforted under all God's dealings with them, knowing

ing that he will make all things work together for their good. And accordingly we read in scripture of his having never failed them, who leaned upon him for help. When they were visited with sickness, or poverty or any other affliction, he enabled them to bear his fatherly correction without murmuring or repining. When sin cries aloud for vengeance, and justice draws the sword, and cuts off the inhabitants of the earth with a swift destruction, then believers happily experience that their gracious God in the midst of wrath remembers mercy. His judgments upon his enemies are mercies to them. When the earth quakes and trembles under their feet, their soul does not melt away because of the trouble. The rock upon which they stand cannot be moved, and therefore in the midst of the earthquake, they can triumphantly say, " God is our refuge " and strength, a very present help in trou- " ble, therefore will not we fear, though " the earth be removed, and though the " mountains be carried into the midst of the " sea." Would not you think yourselves happy if this was your case? And yet believers have still a greater happiness. When death itself approaches it is welcome: for

the

the sting of death is taken out, and they have no fear left about any thing, but sin. They are more afraid of sin, than of poison. They would not live in sin to gain the world, and in the strength of their beloved Saviour on whom they lean and rely, they can and do conquer sin, so that it does not reign in their mortal bodies. What do you think of the safety and happiness of those persons, who are afraid of nothing, but of offending their reconciled Father? Certainly they are the happiest men upon earth; and every sinner would envy them, if the devil had not propagated an opinion that they are all under a delusion. If any of you, my brethren, have entertained this opinion, weigh the matter carefully, and you will find this makes nothing for your case. For what you suppose to be delusion is a sweet and comfortable state of mind, promised in the word of God, and bestowed upon the children of God; and are they deluded, think ye, who say they have received nothing more than what God had promised to give? That faith, by which ye suppose us deluded, does certainly free us from the commission of many sins, and from many of the miseries of the present life, and it deludes us into a kind of fortitude, that not only enables us to bear reproach, contempt, injuries, and

afflictions,

afflictions, but alſo to rejoice under them, when we meet them for following Chriſt. Oh happy deluſion! We are deluded into a ſtrong belief that God loves us in Jeſus Chriſt, and therefore we are confident, that whatever he appoints for us is the beſt. Be it poverty, or ſickneſs, or any outward evil, we can reſign ourſelves contentedly to his holy will, being aſſured that our loving Father would ſend us nothing, but what will be for our good. Is all this a deluſion? Can a man be deluded into ſuch real ſolid happineſs? Glory be to God, I have taſted a little of it, and I would not part with the bleſſing for a thouſand worlds. Upon this earth there is no happineſs like it. Heaven only exceeds it. Therefore you gain nothing by giving credit to the devils lie. He would have you to believe that all God's people are under a deluſion, and that they only fancy they are ſafe and happy by leaning upon Jeſus Chriſt. And can you believe this barefaced lie? Who but the father of lies could raiſe ſuch an evil report upon the good land, and who but his children would give any credit to it? For the ſpirit of truth ſpeaks a different language. Hear what he has promiſed, and then judge, whether we are deluded, who ſay, he has fulfilled his promiſe to us: " Thou wilt
" keep

"keep him in perfect peace whose mind is stayed on thee, because he trusteth in thee. Trust ye in the Lord for ever: for in the Lord Jehovah is everlasting strength." Here he engages to keep those persons in perfect peace by his everlasting strength, whose minds are stayed upon him. Fear then, careless sinner, to call this perfect peace a delusion: for thereby thou wouldest ascribe to the devil the glory of God's work; but rather ask God to shew thee thy guilt and wretchedness, that thou mayest find thy want of that peace which God has to give. Hast thou no desire to ask? If thou canst not send up one wish for it, may his good Spirit now put it into thy heart. Oh that thou couldst pray to be in the happy state of the faithful soul, " Coming up from the wilderness leaning upon her beloved." And to every one who desires to be in this state I make my *second* remark.

I suppose you begin to find the heavy burden of sin, and it is growing intolerable; then look to Christ, that he may take it upon him, and ease you. He can sustain it; for he hath borne the weight of the sins of the world, and he will ease you of your burden, whenever you can cast it upon the Lord.

Lord. But if you are discouraged from trusting in him, and find your sins to be so many and so great, that you fear he will not receive you: fear not. Be your sins ever so heinous, if you are sensible of them, and can ask mercy, he will be merciful. He never shut any one out of mercy because he was a great sinner. The greatest have found mercy, and so may you, if you go as one of the greatest to ask it. Ask, and ye shall have. Pray to Jesus for his help, and he will raise you up. Pray for faith, and he will enable you to lean upon him for wisdom, and righteousness, and holiness, and eternal redemption.

But you have, you say, been praying and waiting upon him, and yet you find nothing but coldness and deadness in your heart. You make no progress. Though you desire to lean upon Christ every step, yet you cannot put your whole trust and confidence in him, your mind is full of so many doubts and fears. Several persons, when they first set out in the ways of religion, get into this temper. They are always disputing and doubting, whether this step be right, and that service accepted, looking too much into their own hearts, and looking too little at Christ, and so they puzzle and perplex themselves,

themselves, and can gain no ground. If you would be freed from these difficulties, follow the light which God gives, and make use of the help which he offers; and that is the way to receive more. You, my brethren, are seeking his promised salvation. Enquire, what you are to trust to, and to rest upon at present. If God has made a provision for your case, it ought to be your support. And has he not left you the word of promise to rely upon? He has commanded you, and it is your bounden duty, to believe the report which God has given of his Son. You are required to take him at his word, and to believe, that Christ is, as the scripture has set him forth, a Saviour willing and able to save every sinner, who comes unto him. This is the scripture character of Christ; and if you do not believe what it says concerning him, you make God a liar. And you will call in question both the faithfulness and the goodness of God, if you think that he has promised any thing to them that seek, which he will not fulfil to you who are seeking. Heaven and earth shall pass away, but not one tittle of God's promises shall pass away, until all be fulfilled.

Is not this then, my brethren, the point wherein you fail? You are seeking Christ,

and

and his salvation, but you want something more than the word of promise, before you rest upon it in the manner God requires. You desire a particular application of the promises, and want the experience of them, before you can wholly rely upon the faithfulness and truth of God who made them. Examine, whether this be not the case; and if it be, consider how you discredit the word of God. You are commanded to believe it, and unless you think God is a liar, you may safely rely upon it. It is your duty to receive Christ, as he is there set forth, and to wait for the witness of the Spirit in the application of Christ, when and in what manner he shall think proper to give it you. And suppose your belief of his word of promise, your faith of reliance, may be very weak, yet however bring it into act. Let it operate. Lean upon Jesus Christ, as well as you are enabled, and you will certainly go on lamely perhaps at first, but however halt on, and believe that he pities you, and lay the care of bringing you safely through upon him. Don't lie complaining and arguing, but believe his word, and act faith upon the word of promise, and the Lord shall be with you. And the weaker you find yourself, you have the more need to rely upon Christ.

Look

Look more at him, and less at yourself, and wait humbly upon him, and you will not long want his promised comfort. He will give you joy and peace in believing, and shew you that you are in the happy number of the redeemed of the Lord, to whom I make my *third* and *last* remark.

My Christian brethren, you have experienced the truth of the doctrine in the text, and you know the happiness of leaning with faith upon Christ. You are enabled to trust the whole of your salvation on him. In all your duties you lean upon him. You hear, and read the word, and pray, and give alms, and attend at the Lord's table, not to make yourselves righteous in the sight of God. This is not your motive. You know that he who made your persons righteous, must also make your duties acceptable. He, that justified you, is the same also that must sanctify you. Nothing can make you holy, but his good Spirit. To this you trust. And as he has promised that his grace shall at all times be sufficient for you, you can therefore lean upon Jesus in the worst of times, and the sorest trials. The more you are afflicted, the more do you rely upon him, and cleave the closer to him, and therefore
the

the stronger you grow. Sickness cannot weaken your hold; death itself cannot break it off: " for when I walk through the valley " of the shadow of death, says the *Psalmist,* " then thou art my support, then thy rod " and thy staff comfort me:" leaning upon thee I neither fear death, nor him that hath the power of death.

The text thus explained and applied teaches us one of the most useful lessons for the conduct of life. All men are seeking happiness, but few find it; because they seek it where it is not. It has been a general enquiry among thinking men, how they might be able to bear up under afflictions, how they might keep the mind easy when the body was in pain and sickness, and how they might be happy in all circumstances; but upon the principles of moral philosophy they could never fortify the mind against the evils of life. Various remedies were proposed, but they all failed, when they were brought to the trial. But the great secret is revealed in my text. If you would be always happy, lean upon Christ; take off all trust and confidence from every other object, and place them upon Christ. It is a command, " Cast " all your care upon him," he will bear it for you; but in order to do this, you muſt know by faith that "he careth for you"—for how can you truſt yourſelf and all your affairs in his hands, unleſs you have ſome evidence of his love to you? But when you receive faith from the gift, and from the operation of God, and thereby know your intereſt in the promiſes made through Chriſt, and, as our church expreſſes it, are aſſured of the favour and goodneſs of God towards you, then you can lean upon him for his promiſed help. And this faith can carry you ſafely through all troubles and temptations, be they ever ſo great, becauſe it is almighty. Faith does not attack them in the ſtrength of nature, but in the omnipotence of grace. It relies upon the promiſe of God, and believes that it ſhall be done according to his word. When faith can thus plead the promiſes and lean upon Chriſt for the fulfilling them, it will certainly receive whatever is promiſed — power to ſubdue ſin — power to live unto God — grace ſufficient to reſiſt temptations — comfort under afflictions — ſtrength in the inner man when the body is in pain and ſickneſs — and victory over the laſt enemy death: " for all things are poſſible " to him that believeth."

Here then is the infallible scripture remedy for the evils of life. May the Lord God dispose all your hearts to take it. If you would be safe and happy, lean upon Christ. But if there be any of you, my brethren, who are still determined to lean upon some other thing for happiness, be assured it will deceive you in the end. You may seem to go on smoothly and merrily for a while, but there is a day coming, when you will see the falseness of your confidence. In the day of sickness, in the day of death, and much more in the great day of judgment, you will have nothing to support you, unless you lean upon Jesus Christ. Be persuaded then in time to put your whole trust and confidence in him. If you see your want of a Saviour, go to him, and he will supply all your wants. Ask and seek the precious gift of faith, until you are able to turn your backs upon all worldly happiness, and to come up from the wilderness leaning upon your beloved Jesus. And whenever the grace of God brings you into this happy state, you will then go on in your christian course sweetly and cheerfully. You will find the presence of your God with you every step, and being mightily strengthened with his Spirit in the inner man, the work of salvation will prosper in your souls. Oh that we may be all strong in the Lord, and in the power of his might to travel on in his strength. May every one of you, who has come up from the wilderness of the world to the house of the Lord this day, be enabled to lean and rely upon Christ for his promised help, and may receive out of his fulness grace for grace. If you have never yet been united to him by saving faith, God grant his good Spirit may bless this discourse, and make it the means of uniting you to Jesus Christ. And if you be now united, Oh may you find the bond of union growing stronger and stronger every day, until death perfect it, and eternity continue it in endless bliss and glory. We look up unto thee, O most gracious God, for these blessings, and we ask them in that excellent form of prayer which our church has taught us to use this day. Enable us to pray in faith, while we say,

"O Lord, we beseech thee to keep thy "church and houshold continually in thy "true religion, that they who do lean only "upon the hope of thy heavenly grace, "may evermore be defended by thy mighty "power, through Jesus Christ our Lord. "Amen." *Fifth Sunday after the Epiphany.*

SERMON XI.

Chap. viii. Ver. 6, 7.

Set me as a seal upon thine heart, as a seal upon thine arm: for love is strong as death, jealousy is cruel as the grave, the coals thereof are coals of fire, which hath a most vehement flame. Many waters cannot quench love, neither can the floods drown it: if a man would give all the substance of his house for love, it would utterly be contemned,

THIS song of loves, which treats of the pure and spiritual affection between Christ and the believer, is very little understood. Worldly and sensual men read it with worldly and sensual tempers, and therefore find nothing divine in it. It is to such persons of all scripture the most exceptionable: and no wonder. St. *Paul* gives us the reason,

reason, " The natural man, fays he, dif-
" cerneth not the things of the Spirit of
" God, neither can he know them, becaufe
" they are fpiritually difcerned:" for want
of this fpiritual difcernment, he cannot fee
the things of the Spirit of God treated of
in this divine fong. But it is neverthelefs
a fine painting, although thefe blind men
cannot judge of it. The fubject is the union
of Chrift with the believer. He that is not
a believer does not know what it is to be
united to Chrift; and therefore he is as
incapable of judging of this poem as a blind
man is of the expreffion of a beautiful picture.
But he that has the love of Chrift in his heart,
who is one with Chrift and Chrift with him,
he knows what the believer means, when
fpeaking to Chrift in the text, he fays, " Set
" me as a feal upon thine heart, as a feal
" upon thine arm: for love is ftrong as
" death, jealoufy is cruel as the grave, the
" coals thereof are coals of fire, which hath
" a moft vehement flame. Many waters
" cannot quench love, neither can the
" floods drown it: if a man would give
" all the fubftance of his houfe for love, it
" would utterly be contemned." This is
the believers prayer. He has tafted of the
loving

loving kindnefs of his Lord. The Holy Ghoſt had ſhed abroad the love of Chriſt in his heart, and he could truly ſay, " I love " him, becauſe he firſt loved me." He was happy in the enjoyment of his Lord's love; but he wanted more, as every one does who has taſted of it. He hungered and thirſted for more full experience of it, and earneſtly prayed to be rooted and grounded in love, that he might be able to comprehend what is the breadth, and length, and depth, and height, and to know the love of Chriſt that paſſeth knowledge. The believer knew it was his intereſt to ſtudy this love, and to try to take ſome dimenſions of it, although it ſurpaſs all human underſtanding, yea the underſtanding of all ſaints, of angels and glorified ſpirits, to comprehend it fully; but the more he did comprehend, the happier he found himſelf. When he confidered the wonders of Chriſt's love in his humiliation, in his life, in his ſufferings, in his death, in his refurrection, and afcenfion, and in the glories of his mediatorial kingdom, he found particular ſweetneſs in this confideration, that he had an intereſt in all the good offices of this love. He knew, that whatever it did for finners was done for him. An would not this greatly recommend the study of Christ's love above all other studies: for how exceedingly delightful must it be to trace out the steps of his love, since every new discovery is a fresh addition to the believer's happiness? Upon this experimental plan the speaker in the text considered the subject. He prays for a more full and perfect enjoyment of Christ's love, and urges his petition by several motives taken from what Christ did and suffered for sinners. He takes a view of the triumphs of his love in the greatness of his actions and sufferings, and then by them pleads with him for a more abundant measure of love. May the divine Spirit enable every one of you to put up the same prayer. May he shed abroad in your hearts that love, which will make your consideration of this scripture useful and profitable. Under his guidance then let us enquire

First, Into the sense and meaning of the words, and

Secondly, Into the practical use we can make of them.

This

This divine song is drawn up in the manner of a dialogue. The speakers are Christ and the church. The church is every faithful soul, which is united to Christ as the members are to the body, or the branches to the vine. When some men hear the word church, they are apt to apply it to national or congregational assemblies; but the scripture applies it to believers, and to them only, allowing none to be true members, not even of any christian communion, unless they be members of Christ's mystical body.—And our reformers in the 19th article give us this definition of the visible church — " It is a con-
" gregation of faithful men, in which the
" pure word of God and the sacraments be
" duly administered." One of these faithful men (for of numbers of them a church is composed) is here expressing the fervent prayer of his heart, to have more full experience of Christ's love. He had no doubt of the favour and goodness of God towards him in Christ. He had received many clear proofs of it. He had the scripture marks and evidences in his own soul of Christ's being his beloved and his friend; and he was happy in knowing this. The sense of Christ's love to him had enabled him to love Christ in return,

return, and therefore he was led to pray for the continuance, and for the increase of Christ's love — " Set me as a seal upon thine " heart;" and convey to me under thy seal all the graces and blessings which thy love has to give: for the foundation of God standeth sure, having this seal, The Lord knoweth them that are his; he knoweth them that have his seal upon them, O seal me then for thine. When a man sets his hand and seal to a will or to a deed of gift, it is as if he should declare, This is my last will and testament, this is my act and deed. So when Christ sets the believer as a seal upon his heart, it is as if he should declare — I seal this person for mine, and give unto him freely all the benefits of the new testament in my blood, and this is properly attested by my word and by my Spirit. The word is the outward witness, the Spirit applying the word is the inward witness. The scripture very clearly assigns to him the office of sealing believers, as *Eph.* i. 13. " After " that ye believed in Christ, ye were sealed " with the Holy Spirit of promise;" and chap. iv. 30. " Grieve not the Holy Spirit " of God, by whom ye are sealed unto the " day of redemption." Christ redeemed

both

both our real and perfonal eftate, but we are not in poffeffion of either, until it be conveyed to us under the feal of the Holy Spirit. Chrift's redemption without the Holy Spirit's application, is like a deed without a feal, which you know can legally convey nothing. It is the figning and fealing that makes it good in law. And when the Holy Spirit feals the believer, then he receives the earneft of his inheritance. The believer in the text had this earneft in himfelf, and therefore he prayed fervently for a greater meafure of Chrift's love; and he prayed the more fervently, as well from the lively remembrance he had of his former mifery, while he was without Chrift in the world, as from the pleafing fenfe of his prefent happinefs. All the time his heart had been fet upon the world, he remembered in what a vain fhadow he had been walking, and how he had difquieted himfelf in vain. From whatever he fought happinefs, he was difappointed; and therefore convinced of the emptinefs of every creature-comfort, and of the finfulnefs of refting in them — having found the beft of them unable to fill the defires of his foul, he had turned from the creature to God: God had every thing to give

give that could make him completely happy, and God the Saviour was willing to give it. As his power is, so is his love; they are alike infinite. The speaker in the text had happy experience of Christ's love, and did not doubt of his power to save. With a grateful sense of what Christ had already done, he prayed that the Holy Spirit would make him increase and abound in love. My brethren, is this your prayer? Do you know so much of his love to you, as to pray for more love to him? If you are not seeking happiness in his love, in what have you been seeking it all your life, or in what are you now seeking it? Out of Christ you could seek it in nothing but in the sinful love of the creature. And now ask yourselves what you have found? If you deal honestly with your souls, you must confess that you have met with continual disappointments. And why then will you not be wise from experience? Are you tired and weary of the dull round of worldly joys? Then pray the Holy Spirit to turn your affections from these deluding objects to the Lord Jesus, and when your hearts are set upon him, he will then make you perfectly, eternally blessed. Blessedness is his to give. The world has it not. Oh

turn

turn then from it to our loving God, and beg you may know so much of his love as to be able to pray with the believer in the text that Christ would " set you as a seal up-" on his heart," and let you know your interest in his love. When you are sealed for *his*, and find his affections are placed upon you, then you will have the comfortable enjoyment of his present graces, and sure and certain hope of your inheriting the promises of eternal life: for then he will also " set you " as a seal upon his arm." His arm is his power. The hand is the active part of the body, by which the strength of it is exerted. We labour and work with our hands; and when the scripture speaks of the arm of the Lord, it means his active power, which the faithful soul here desires may be exercised continually for its salvation. To be as a seal upon his heart would be of no use, without the seal upon his arm. His love would not be a blessing, unless it was an active operative love. But it is therefore desirable to partake of Christ's love, because it will always awake the arm of the Lord, and will bring salvation. His love and his power are never separated; his heart and his arm act together, and therefore the believing soul does not put
them

them asunder, but prays in the text, that the beloved Saviour would give her experience of both — " O set me as a seal
" upon thy heart, that whatever thy love
" disposes thee to do for sinners, I may share
" and partake in it — Oh set me also as a
" seal upon thine arm, let me also, blessed
" Jesus, be engraven upon the palms of thy
" hands, that in all thy works thou mayest
" remember me with mercy. Let thy love
" engage thy power to make all things work
" together for my good."

These are the desires of the faithful in the text; and they are the fervent desires of every true believer. And if there be any of you, who are not convinced that these are the breathings of true faith, then you are ignorant of the nature of Christ's love. You know it not, because you have had no experience of it. If you had ever found your want of his love, and had ever tasted of it, you would bear your testimony to the truth of the following description, *viz.* " That his
" love is strong as death, the ardor of it is
" harder than the grave, the coals thereof
" are coals of fire, which hath a most ve-
" hement flame, burning with such an
" in-

" inextinguishable affection, that many wa-
" ters could not quench it, neither could the
" floods drown it, and of so inestimable a
" price, that if a man should think of buy-
" ing it, or of meriting it, and would give
" all the substance of his house for it, it
" would utterly be despised." These are
the excellencies of Christ's love, for which
the faithful soul so earnestly desired farther
experience of it, and for which you will desire it with the same earnestness, as soon as
you are made sensible of your wants. When
you find the misery of sin, and the wretched
slavery of serving satan, and the world, and
the flesh, who have no wages to give you
but death, then you will wish your souls
under the protection of that love, which is
" strong as death." The love of Christ was
stronger than death: for he conquered death,
and took out its sting. And the sting of
death will be taken out of your conscience,
when it is sprinkled with his atoning blood.
His love brought him down from heaven,
and he took a body of flesh, in which he
might obey and suffer and die. Accordingly
he became obedient, obedient unto death,
even the death of the cross. He died the
painful, ignominious, and accursed death of
the

the cross. Greater love hath no man than this, that a man lay down his life for his friend; but how far does the love of Jesus exceed this instance; he laid down his life, not for friends but for sinners, for enemies, the bitterest enemies, who persecuted him even unto death — He died for his persecutors. Greater love than this there cannot be: for as he died to save his enemies from death, so he rose again, that they might rise to a newness of life, whereby he shewed " his love to be stronger than the grave." Our translation reads, *jealousy* is cruel as the grave—The word rendered jealousy denotes the ardor and intenseness of Christ's love, not what he thought of the love of others to him, but the nature of his love to them, the great degree, the flaming ardor and intenseness of it, which made him submit not only to death, but also to go down to the grave. In the prison of the grave, the bodies of all the dead were shut up. The prison was secured with bars and gates, and guarded by him that had the power of death, and he had suffered not one prisoner for four thousand years to escape. To this prison the Lord Jesus went down, and he was detained in it for three days: but it was not possible
that

that he should be holden any longer. On the third day he broke through the gate of death, and demonstrated that his love was stronger than the grave. And when he is describing his victory to the beloved apostle, he represents it under a very beautiful image. " I am he that liveth, says he, and was " dead, and behold I am alive for evermore, " Amen, and have the keys of hell and of " death." My brethren, are any of you afraid to die? Has death still a sting, and the grave victory over you? If they have, did you ever consider what was the reason? Is it not because you either do not believe that Christ has the keys of death and the grave in his hands, or else you have no certainty that he will use them for your interest? You have no knowledge of Christ's love to you. The Holy Ghost never shed it abroad in your heart, perhaps you never desired it, and therefore you are ignorant of his having died and risen from the grave for your salvation. If you knew your interest in his death, and had experienced the power of his resurrection, you would no longer fear death and the grave: for then faith would enable you to triumph over both. You would have nothing to fear, but every thing blessed to hope for

for from them, after you knew that Chrift had fet you as a feal upon his heart, and as a feal upon his arm: for then death and the grave, inftead of feparating you from the love of God which is in Chrift Jefus our Lord, would bring you to the more full and eternal enjoyment of it.

My brethren, if you have not this love, do you defire it? Can you pray for it? If the Holy Spirit has difcovered to you your want of it, and has put you upon afking, afk, and he will grant you your heart's defire. You fhall know Chrift, and the power of his refurrection, know him to be your Saviour and your God. And this experience of his love to you, will open to your underftanding the next words in the defcription, *viz.* that the ardor of Chrift's love is like coals of fire burning clear and bright with a moft vehement flame, " fuch as many " waters could not quench." Thefe many waters are the many troubles he met with, and they were fo many, that they would have quenched any love but his. He went through a fea of troubles from the manger to the crofs, but his love burnt all the time with fuch a vehement flame, that the many

waters

waters he waded through could not quench it. *Herod* perfecuted him, while a child, and forced him to flee his country, but his love to his enemies brought him back. His very humiliation, until he entered on his public miniftry, was a great trial. As God he was the higheft in heaven, as man he was one of the loweft on earth—That was confequently the higheft love which ftooped the loweft to fave finners. You may read in the Gofpels the hiftory of the many troubles he went through. His public life was one continued fcene of oppofition. Trouble came, like wave after wave, raging and lifting up their heads on high, but the ardor of his love mounted and flamed above them all. You know, that nothing cools love fo much as meeting with hatred; he was hated, even for doing good, and yet he loved his enemies. They poured cold water upon his love, by railing at his doctrine, blafpheming his perfon, blafpheming his miracles, but his love, being of an uncommon nature, burnt the brighter. He went on doing good to his revilers and his blafphemers. And though the rulers and nation of the *Jews*, a few poor people excepted, would not receive him for their promifed Meffiah, yet thefe many waters could not quench his love. It burnt with a pure flame, which neither the ingratitude nor the vile treatment of mankind could in the leaſt damp, or abate. And we need not wonder that many waters could not quench, " for the floods could not drown the love " of Chriſt." It ſtill kept its ardor, when the overflowing flood broke over his head. When the floods of ungodly men roſe up againſt him, and tried his love with every pain and reproach, which is diſtreſſing to human nature, they only ſerved to make his love ſhine out the purer and brighter. In his laſt ſufferings theſe floods tried to drown his love, but it mounted up triumphant above all. In the garden on the eve of the paſſion he had a proſpect of what he was to undergo, and as there was no other way for man to be ſaved, but for him to drink the bitter cup, he therefore reſolved to take it, and to drink it up to the very dregs. No ſooner had he ſpoken the words, " Father thy will be " done," but the cup was inſtantly put into his hands. He is apprehended, and all his diſciples forſake him. Not one, not *Peter* himſelf, durſt own him. As a malefactor he is brought before the high-prieſt, accuſed for ſaying he was the ſon of God, ſhamefully

fully intreated and spit upon, blindfolded by way of insult on his prophetical office, and struck upon the face, led to *Pilate*, tried and acquitted, and yet whipt and scourged, crowned with thorns by way of insult on his regal office, and the thorns driven into his head by the barbarous soldiers until the blood ran down his temples, and then innocent, and pronounced so by his judge, nevertheless given up to the rage of the people—to the floods of ungodly men that went about to devour him. They thirsted for his blood, and shed it as if it had been water. Having gotten him into their power, they led him out, marking the way as he went with his blood, and having reached mount *Calvary*, there they prepare their instruments of death. They drive the nails through his hands and feet, fastening his body to the cross, and then lifting up the cross they stand by to insult and blaspheme him. O love divine, how triumphantly didst thou rise above all these floods of opposition, when that sweet prayer came out of thy dying mouth, " Father, forgive " them, for they know not what they do." But he had another flood of opposition to withstand, infinitely more dreadful than the former;

former; he had the wrath and justice of his Father to sustain, who finding all our sins upon him, took full satisfaction, even to the uttermost farthing. His Father had before declared by a voice from heaven, "This is my beloved Son in whom I am well pleased:" but now his justice draws the sword in wrath upon his beloved Son. Whence was this? What! is there any variableness or shadow of turning in God? No. He was still the beloved Son of the Father, but he was made sin for us who knew no sin: he was wounded for our transgressions, and was bruised for our iniquities; he bore our griefs and carried our sorrows, from the time he sweat as it were great drops of blood in the garden, until he expired upon the cross. And what he endured while that scripture was fulfilling, " Awake, O sword, " against my shepherd, and against the man " that is my fellow, faith the Lord," and justice was taking full and perfect satisfaction for sin upon him, no tongue can tell, no imagination can conceive. He says himself, " All thy waves and storms are gone over " me." They broke upon his head, and with so much fury, that he complains in the 88th *Psalm*, ver. 7. " Thine indignation
" lyeth

"lyeth hard upon me, and thou haft vexed me with all thy ftorms." When all the waves and ftorms of the Father's wrath, which fhould have fallen upon us, vexed him, he might well fay, " Was there ever forrow like unto my forrow, wherewith the Lord hath afflicted me in the day of his fierce anger." There never was any forrow like that, which occafioned this lamentation, " My God, my God, why haft thou forfaken me?" All the powers in heaven and earth heard this cry, and were affected with it—the fun hid his face —there was darknefs over the whole earth —the rocks were rent—the graves opened— the dead arofe—the veil of the temple was rent from the top to the bottom. What the bleeding Lamb of God fuffered at this time furpaffeth human underftanding. But however, in this day of the Lord's fierce anger, the floods of divine wrath did not drown our Lord's love. He bore up under all, until love heard the happy words—*It is finifhed*, and then he bowed his head, and gave up the ghoft. But his love did not die. No. It gained the greateft victory in death. We read of *Samfon*, that the dead, whom he flew at his death, were more than those whom he slew in his life—which was a type and figure of the great victory, which Christ obtained by his death; for he then vanquished all the enemies of our peace. His love was stronger than death: because through death he overcame death, and him that had the power of death. It was stronger than the grave, for he redeemed his own body before it had seen corruption. And he arose from the grave as the first fruits of the dead, and behold he has in his hands the keys of hell and of death, so that neither death nor hell shall have any power over them that believe in him. And being risen from the dead, and ascended into heaven, he is seated upon the throne of glory, and he neither wants love nor power to bestow upon them that believe in him, every grace, and every blessing which can make them happy in time and in eternity.

Surely then, the love of Christ is beyond all value. What price can you set upon it? Might not the faithful with good reason say of it in the text, " If a man would give all " the substance of his house for this love, it " would utterly be despised," for it is a free love, it cannot be bought. It is inestimable, and

and the riches of it are unsearchable. With what can you think of purchasing it? With the substance of a man's house? Why, it is one of the free gifts of this love, and can you then think of meriting or buying it with its own gifts? This love created all things that are in heaven and that are in earth, so that you have nothing to offer it but what is already its own. And if you are one of the Lord's people, it redeemed you from the bondage of sin and satan, of death and the grave, and you have only to receive its blessings, and to be thankful: for you yourself, and all that you have, are not your own. You are bought with a price. And what can you offer the Lord, but what is already his own? His by right of creation, by right of redemption doubly his. And must he not then utterly despise both you and your gifts, if you think that the substance of your house is to be compared with his love? He will despise you, and you will feel his resentment through the ages of eternity, if you disparage his love so much, as to think that any thing in the world, yea the whole world itself, ought to be put in competition with his love. They who have tasted of it, know it to be invaluable. The least experience of it is

worth

worth thousands of worlds. And Oh that he who has it to give may now shed it abroad in all your hearts, that you may feel the happiness of it. May this be the desire of every soul here present—Set me, Lord Jesus, as a seal upon thine heart, set me as a seal upon thine arm, for thy love to sinners is strong as death, the ardor of it is mightier than the grave—it burnt like bright coals of fire, which hath a most vehement flame, many waters could not quench thy love, nor could the floods drown it. If a man would give all the substance of his house to purchase thy love, he and his gifts would be utterly despised.

My brethren, can you make use of this prayer? Are these the pious breathings of your souls? You have heard from the sense of the words, that these were the pious breathings of the faithful under the *Old Testament*, and they must be yours under the *New* if you would experience the comforts of the doctrine in the text, and to stir you up to seek them is the subject of my *second* general head: under which I shall make two or three short practical inferences.

The

The first relates to the manner, in which the words are drawn up. They are in the form of a prayer, founded upon past experience of Christ's love, and earnestly desiring a larger share of it. And is this your heart's desire? Can you willingly and heartily pray to have the love of other objects shut out of your hearts, and to find your happiness in the love of Christ, and in being sealed for his? If you can pray thus, may you daily find more reason to love Jesus Christ. But if you cannot, is it not expedient that you should consider what is the reason? For has not Jesus Christ every perfection in himself, and every grace and blessing to give, which ought to draw the affections of miserable sinners unto himself? And yet you have no love for him. What is the cause, which makes you act so directly against your own interest? Is it not an unlawful attachment to the world, or to some object in it, which you set up against Christ? You prefer it to him. You think it can make you happier than he can, and so you give up your hearts to its service. Herein you are guilty of a monstrous absurdity? because you prefer creature-comforts to God; and you are guilty of monstrous wickedness, because you
leave

leave God to idolize the creature. And though after daily experience you find, that the creature cannot make you happy, yet still you idolize it. What prodigious power must sin have over a man, how entirely must it have blinded his understanding, when it can make him act against the clearest evidence, even of his own senses? for upon whatever object you place your hearts, in preference, or in opposition to Christ, it cannot make you happy: for this plain reason, because you sin in giving that love to it, which is due to him. " My son, says he, give " ME thy heart." I will make thee happy by taking guilt out of thy conscience, by pardoning thee freely, and shedding the love of God abroad in thy heart. Until this be done, no creature can make you happy. While sin is unpardoned, while guilt is in the conscience, and while the broken law condemns, what can money, what can pleasure, what can honour give of happiness? They may for a time sooth the uneasiness of the mind, but they cannot remove it. Nothing can remove it, but Jesus Christ. He has perfect peace to give. And if ever you obtain it, you must receive it from his free love and bounty.

My

My brethren, do you give your assent to these truths? How do they appear to you? Do they not carry conviction along with them? Certainly they do, unless men be entirely blinded with sin. If they have convinced you, and you begin to desire to know the love of Christ, then turn from seeking happiness in creature-comforts, where it cannot be found, and seek it in Jesus Christ, and you will find in him true solid bliss, when he sets you as a seal upon his heart, and as a seal upon his arm. But if you have not been convinced from what has been said, then turn to the world, and get its seal upon your hearts. If the world can make you happier than God can, idolize it. Serve it, as too many do, with every faculty of soul and body, and pay it that obedience which is due to God only. But did you ever consider, who is the god of this world, that ruleth in the children of disobedience? Is it not that old serpent, called the devil and satan, who deceiveth the whole world? And what! would you be found, when you come to die, with the devils seal upon you? Do you now deliberately choose to be marked for his, and to have your portion with him in the lake that burneth with fire and brimstone for ever and

and ever? If there be any of you thus far deluded and infatuated, let me entreat you to read the 9th chapter of *Ezekiel*. You will there find a lively image of your prefent ftate; I pray God to make it the means of fhewing you your danger. The Lord gives a command to flay young and old, and to deftroy the whole city; but firft one cloathed in linen goes to fet a mark upon the Lord's people, and they only were to be faved. You have not the Lord's mark upon you, therefore in the day of his fierce anger his eye will not fpare, neither will he have pity. Whenever the deftroying angel is fent out, he has no power to hurt the fervants of God, who are fealed; as you may read, *Rev.* vii. Four angels had a commiffion to hurt the earth, and the fea, but they were not to execute it until the Lord's people were fealed, then they were to deftroy and fpare not. Are not thefe awful fcriptures? Have not they made you fenfible of your prefent danger? May the Spirit of the living God apply them. Oh may his grace now begin to work upon your hearts! Now may he put it into your minds from a due fenfe of your wants to feek a fupply from the love of Chrift, that you may receive profit from what I have to remark upon

upon the second part of the text, *viz*. the greatness of Christ's love.

But of this you can form no judgment, unless you have seen your guilt and your misery, and found how much you stood in need of his love. It will appear great in proportion, as you find your want of it, and greater as you experience it. In itself it is divine and infinite. It partakes of the nature of its author. It is, like him, above all blessing and praise. If you try to take the dimensions of it, you will conclude with the apostle, that it surpasseth knowledge, yea the knowledge of angels as well as of men; the heigth, the depth, the length, the breadth of it cannot be measured by any created being. Oh the height and depth of that love, which brought our divine Lord from the highest heavens to the lowest humiliation. Oh the length of that love which reaches as far as the east is from the west, for so far hath he set our sins from us. Oh the breadth of it, which includes a great multitude, that no man could number, of all nations, and kindreds, and people, and tongues. But although Christ's love be thus unspeakably great, and inconceivably divine, yet until you feel the misery of sin, you will not think of applying to Christ for his love. But when

when guilt torments, death terrifies, the grave and hell appear to you in all their horrors, then you will think it a blessing indeed, if you could have that love in your hearts, which is able to cast out these fears. And the knowledge of Christ's love to you casteth out all fear: for his love has conquered all your enemies, and is now almighty to conquer them in you. For sin he has made an atonement, death he has subdued, and him that had the power of death, he is risen from the grave as the first fruits of the dead, and has opened the gate of everlasting life. O beseech him then to let you share in that love, which was stronger than death, mightier than the grave; whereby all his conquests shall be yours. When you are united to him in the bonds of love, he will make you more than conqueror. He will make your love triumphant like his. He will so strengthen it, that many waters shall not be able to quench it, neither shall the floods be able to drown it. Neither distress nor persecution, neither life nor death, neither the pleasures of the world nor the temptations of the devil, shall be able to separate you from the love of Christ Jesus your Lord.

If you see your want of this love, seek, and you shall find it. The promise is—" They that seek me early shall find me." And if any of you have been seeking and have not found, you may conclude, that you have been seeking wrong—and have not followed the last part of the text, *viz.* seeking it as a free gift, which with all your endeavours and pains you cannot merit: for such is the free and inestimable love of Christ, that if a man would give all the substance of his house for this love it would utterly be despised. If you had millions of worlds to give, they would be counted as nothing. He would reject you and your worthless bribes—As one said upon a like occasion, " Thy money perish with thee, because thou " hast thought, that the free gift of God was " to be purchased with money." Not only all that thou hast, but also all that thou canst desire, is not to be compared with the love of Christ. Whatever can make the sinner happy in time, whatever can make him blessed in eternity, Christ's love is able to bestow, and does bestow upon those, who find their want of it, and who come humbled under a sense of their wants, to ask it as a matter of free grace and bounty. It is to the glory of his love,

love, that he bestows upon the unworthy. And if his good Spirit has enabled you to see your want of it, and you can ask it as an unworthy sinner, you will receive it. This is your only qualification, to acknowledge that you do not deserve it. Go to the throne of his grace with this humble temper, hungering and thirsting after righteousness, and the Lord Jesus will send you away filled with good things.

It is evident then from what has been said, that there is perfect happiness to be found in the love of our redeeming God. All that call themselves christians profess their belief of this truth, but the generality of them act in direct opposition to their belief, and are seeking happiness where God has decreed it shall not be found. They try to find it in the world, but are disappointed, and after many disappointments they will not give over the search. Their great love for the world will not suffer them to turn their backs upon it, although it has deceived them so often. They are quite enamoured with its fancied goods, and place their whole hearts and affections upon its money, its pleasures, and its honours: these they pursue eagerly,

and

and perhaps attain them; they have their heart's defire, and yet they are unhappy. What is the reafon? Becaufe thefe things cannot fatisfy the wants of a finful foul. Sin feperated the foul from God; not only fet them at a diftance from each other, but alfo occafioned enmity between them. The law and juftice of God are of purer eyes than to behold the leaft fin, and therefore he revealed his wrath from heaven againft all unrighteoufnefs and ungodlinefs of men. And until his law and juftice receive full fatisfaction, God the Father will not appear reconciled, nor pardon the finner, who cannot return to God with any love or confidence, and find happinefs in him, until he believe that God is reconciled, and has pardoned him. Now Jefus Chrift is the only Saviour who has pardon of fin to give. His good Spirit can give the finner the knowledge of the pardon of fin, and fhed abroad in his heart all the comforts of God's pardoning love. Then he will know the truth of the defcription in the text. Chrift's love will appear to him as it is there defcribed. He will be able to take up the words, and to ufe them with the fame fpirit, with which they were fpoken in the Song: for he is happy in the love of Chrift, and can truly fay, " I love " him, becaufe he firft loved me, and gave " himfelf for me."

Since thefe things are fo, furely, my beloved brethren, you will not go away refolved ftill to feek happinefs in the love of creature-comforts. You cannot fuppofe, that the world can make you happier than its almighty Creator and Saviour can. If you had it all in your poffeffion, yet there are times when it could be of no fervice. What pleafure could it give you in ficknefs? How could it remove the torments of a guilty confcience? How could it keep off death, or take out its fting? How could it bring you any comfort, if your poor foul fhould appear with all its fins unpardoned at the judgment-feat of Chrift? Alas, in thefe circumftances the world and the things of it cannot give relief. You know they cannot. And why then will you purfue them? Since there is no happinefs to be found in them, and the more you purfue them, the farther will they lead you from true happinefs. Oh turn from the world then, leave it, follow its vain fhadows no longer, nor difquiet yourfelves in vain. No man was ever happy in the

love

love of the world; but every man is happier than the world can make him, who has only accepted the invitation, "Oh come, taste, "and see how gracious the Lord Jesus is;" but he that has tasted, and seen, and is under the care and protection of Christ's love, he is completely happy, even in times of trial and trouble; because Christ is almighty to deliver; and when he does not deliver from affliction, he is able to sanctify it, and to make it work together for good to them that love him. And is not this an happy state? What sinner would not desire it, and what afflicted person would not pray for it? May he, who is able to bring you into it, put it into all your hearts to seek it. Oh that he may send his good Spirit and give every one of you earnest desires to have this scripture fulfilled in your own souls. May this be the language of every soul here present—Set me, blessed Saviour, as a seal upon thine heart, and as a seal upon thine arm, let thy love and thy power act together for my salvation: for thy love is mightier than death, and stronger than the grave, Oh that I may share in these victories of thy love, the vehement ardor of which many waters could not quench, neither could the floods drown it. If a man would give all the substance of his house to buy this love it would utterly be contemned. I have nothing to purchase it with. Give it to me Lord, as a free gift, and to the glory of the giver.

O dear Redeemer, send us away with these good desires in all our hearts, and cherish them, until we know that love of thine, which passeth knowledge, which exceeds all that can be said of it upon earth, and will exceed all that can be said of it in heaven. There will be no end of singing its praises through eternity. Oh may it be your joy and happiness here in time to sing with grateful hearts the praises of redeeming love until Jesus take you to himself, and put more love into your hearts, and fill your mouths with louder songs of praise to Father, Son, and Holy Spirit, the adorable Trinity in Unity, to whom may we all ascribe equal honour and glory, majesty and dominion now, henceforth, and for evermore. *Amen* and *Amen.*

SERMON XII.

Chap. viii. Ver. 14.

Make haste, my beloved, and be thou like to a roe, or to a young hart upon the mountains of spices.

THE church makes this her last request. She desires her beloved to hasten his coming, which under the Old Testament dispensation referred to his coming in the flesh, as under the New it refers to his second coming. But the church of God, both in the Old Testament and the New, expected another coming of Christ, *viz.* his coming in grace. The believers knew that he was to come, and to abide with them, and not as a sojourner, but as an inhabitant, to dwell in their hearts by faith. This was promised them, and this they have always experienced. The words may with great propriety treat of these three advents of our Lord. And I will endeavour

First, To explain them in their full sense, and then

Secondly, To draw some practical observations from them.

The words were spoken before the coming of Christ in the flesh, and supposing they refer to it, they imply great haste and speed. The faithful would have Christ to hasten his coming in the swiftest manner, whereby they express the holy impatience of their affections, which could not endure delay. They longed to see the desire of all nations incarnate. It was their continual wish and prayer, that they might see the day of Christ. Therefore upon the conclusion of the Song, they break off as it were abruptly with this their last request, upon which their hearts were principally set, *make haste, my beloved.*

This was the continual prayer of believers under the Old Testament, which they made not from any doubt of God's faithfulness and truth, but from their earnest desires after the Saviour of the world. They were sensibly convinced of their great want of him. They found sin in themselves—they read in the law

law of the punishment due to sin, which the law had threatened, and justice was bound to inflict, and they knew that they could do nothing to make an atonement to law and justice, therefore they ardently prayed for the coming of the promised Lamb of God who was to take away sin by the sacrifice of himself, and to answer all the demands of law and justice. The first prophecy was sufficiently clear to be a ground for their prayers. God had declared, that the seed of the woman, one born of a woman, should bruise the serpent's head, in which his poison lay, and thereby destroy the power which he had usurped over mankind. The types and services then instituted, which are in sum and substance the same that were afterwards recorded in the written law, tended to explain the first prophecy, and to keep it continually in remembrance. They served as a schoolmaster to lead men to Christ. From them it was certain that the Saviour would come and be made a sacrifice for sin, but the precise time of his coming was not made known in the first ages of the world. This gave men occasion to expect him in every age, until the fixed time of his coming was revealed. And accordingly we find the patriarchs

triarchs before, and the prophets under the law, waiting with eager defires for his coming: As our Lord affured his apoftles, *Matt.* xiii. 17. " Verily I fay unto you, many prophets " and righteous men have defired to fee thefe " things which ye fee and have not feen " them, and to hear thefe things which ye " hear and have not heard them." There were many prophets and righteous men in the church of God as well before the written law as fince, who defired to fee God incarnate, and to hear the gracious words that fhould proceed out of his mouth. *Jacob* was one of thefe prophets and righteous men, and he expreffes all their defires in his own— " I have waited for thy falvation, O Lord." (*Gen.* xlix. 18.) And the prophet *Ifaiah*, fpeaking in his own name, and in the name of the faithful, fays, — " In the way of thy " judgments, O Lord, have we waited for " thee: the defire of our foul is to thy name, and " to the remembrance of thee." And there were always in the church fome waiting for the promifed confolation of *Ifrael*, and efpecially at the time of his appearing in the flefh, fuch as the juft and devout *Simeon*, who when the holy child Jefus was brought into the temple took him up in his arms, and bleffed God

God and said, " Lord, now lettest thou thy servant depart in peace, for mine eyes have seen thy salvation." And this, my brethren, will be your happy case, when your eyes see the salvation of God. When faith gives you a clear view of your interest in the salvation of Jesus Christ, then whenever you die you will depart in peace.

Thus the *Old Testament* saints desired Christ to hasten his coming in the flesh. They wanted to behold his day. They longed to see the great mystery of godliness opened and explained—God manifest in the flesh. In the fulness of time according to their desires he came. He visited us in great humility, and in the form of a servant, but he thought it not robbery to be equal with God: for he required the same faith in himself as in the Father, " Ye believe in God, believe also in me." *John* xiv. 1. He commanded the same divine honour to be paid to him, " All men should honour the Son, even as they honour the Father," (*John* v. 23.) for he is Jehovah, the self-existent God (*John* viii. 24.) which whoever does not believe shall die in his sins. He supported these high claims by appealing to his miracles,

miracles, which were God's testimony to the truth of his words. Hear his own argument upon this very subject. The Jews were going to stone him for saying that he was God. " If I do not the works of my Father be-
" lieve me not; but if I do, though ye be-
" lieve not me, believe the works, that ye
" may know and believe that the Father is
" in me, and I in him." (*John* x. 37, 38.) He did all the works, which the prophets had foretold the promised Immanuel should perform. And after he had fulfilled the scriptures of the *Old Testament*, had suffered all that law and justice required, and had compleated the great work of salvation, he ascended into heaven, and sat down at the right hand of the majesty on high. And we are now according to his most true promise waiting for his second coming. There is a great day, and not far off, when every eye shall see him coming in the clouds of heaven with power and great glory. God had revealed this very early to his servants the prophets: for *Enoch* the seventh from *Adam* prophecied of it, saying, " Behold the
" Lord cometh with ten thousand of his
" saints to execute judgment upon all, and to
" convince all that are ungodly among them
" of

" of all their ungodly deeds, which they
" have ungodly committed, and of all their
" hard speeches, which ungodly sinners have
" spoken against him." In the *New Testament* we have the manner of our Lord's coming to execute judgment, with the process of the last day very particularly described. And it is the wish and prayer of every faithful soul — that he would hasten this his glorious appearing, and accomplish the great things which are to go before it. When the blessed Jesus closes the volume of revelation with this promise, " Surely I come quickly," the faithful reply, " Amen. Even so come, " Lord Jesus." And daily is it in their prayers — *Thy kingdom come.* And they have good reason to desire it; because all that their Lord and Saviour has to do upon the earth will then be compleated. The number of the elect will be perfected, and he will be admired in them. His enemies will be finally subdued. An end will be put to the reign of sin and satan. There will be no more death. Whatever robbed our redeeming God of his glory will be destroyed. Oh how greatly then is this second coming of our Lord to be desired by all his faithful followers and servants, who are described in
scripture

scripture by this character, that they *love his appearing*. They love it first for his sake, because he will then be glorified in his saints, he will then be glorified for the great glory which he will bestow upon them; and they love it also for their own sakes, because then all their wishes and desires will be fulfilled, when they shall see their beloved Saviour face to face. They will have no more prayers or requests to make. When that great day is come, there will be no more complaints, no more wants or necessities, sorrow and sighing will flee away for ever. Our warfare will be ended, our victory compleated. Our crowns shall shine upon our heads with never-fading lustre, our palms of victory shall be ever green. How exceedingly great this happiness will be we cannot fully comprehend at present. However this one circumstance hightens every thing said of it in scripture, namely, that it will be eternal. When we have ascended from judgment with our Lord, he will admit us into his kingdom of glory. After this meeting we shall part no more; but shall ever be with the Lord, praising and adoring his perfections, and being happy in the enjoyment of them to all eternity. And is not all this happiness earnestly

nestly to be desired by them, who have received through faith the earnest of their inheritance? And will it not be much upon their hearts to pray him to hasten his coming, and will not they, who love his appearing, pray for it with great fervency? Our church is very earnest in her prayers: for she teaches us in the *Burial Service* to be continually praying to him, " that it would " please him of his gracious goodness shortly " to accomplish the number of his elect, and " to hasten his kingdom." And he has promised to hear and to answer these prayers: for when he is describing in St. *Matthew* the tribulation of the last days, which shall be greater than any since the beginning of the world to that time, he says that " for the elects sake these days shall be shortened." Amen. So be it Lord Jesus.

My brethren, when you hear of our Lord's second coming how does it affect you? Do you love to think of the day of his great glory? Do you wish and pray for it? Does the solemnity of it strike no terror into your consciences? Is all peace and joy within, when you hear of the suddenness of his coming, and of the general surprize it will be to

a care-a carelefs world? Do you now find no fear, if the laft trump fhould this moment found and you fhould lift up your eyes and fee the God of glory coming in the clouds of heaven attended with all his holy angels? Could you look up with joy, knowing that your redemption draweth nigh? Is your confcience fo purged from dead works that it would not be alarmed, if the air that we breathe being on fire fhould be diffolved, and the elements fhould melt with fervent heat, and the earth alfo and the works that are therein fhould be burnt up? Are you prepared to draw near the judgment-feat with a true heart in full affurance of faith, having your hearts fprinkled from an evil confcience? When you meditate upon the folemn procefs of the laft day, as defcribed by the Judge himfelf, can you fuppofe yourfelf to be in the midft of this awful fcene, and your ftate ready to be determined to all eternity, and have you no fearful apprehenfions about your falvation? If you have none, may he who delivered you from them ftrengthen and eftablifh your faith that you may daily love our Lord, and love his appearing more and more. But if guilty fear does arife in your heart, when you think of the glorious appearing of the great God

and

and our Saviour at the laſt day, this proves that all is not right in your own ſoul. There is a coming of Chriſt in grace, which you have not yet experienced: for if you had, it would have given you that love, which caſteth out all tormenting fear. If Chriſt had come and manifeſted himſelf to you, as your Saviour, if he had awakened you, had pardoned you freely, and given you the witneſs of the Spirit in your heart, enabling you to look upon God as your reconciled Father, Chriſt as your Saviour, and the Holy Spirit as your guide and comforter, then you could have no reaſon to fear. And this coming of Chriſt is the moſt to be deſired, becauſe without this you do not receive the graces and bleſſings of his firſt coming in the fleſh, and therefore are not prepared for his ſecond coming to judgment. What he did and ſuffered in the fleſh is not imputed unto us for righteouſneſs, until it be applied and appropriated. The Holy Spirit muſt come and ſhew us our intereſt in it, he muſt give us preſent ſalvation from the pollution, and the guilt, and the dominion of ſin, and we muſt know and experience this by true faith, before the fear of Chriſt's coming to judgment can be taken out of the conſcience. But when

when Chrift thus dwells in the heart by faith, then being interefted in all the graces of his firft coming, we may wait for the bleffings of his fecond coming with hopes full of immortality. Therefore,

My brethren, above all things feek the experience of Chrift's coming to you in grace: for when you once know and love him as your Saviour, you cannot fear him as your judge: but from the fenfe of his love to you, you will be able with the faithful in the text to call him *your beloved*, and to pray for his fpeedy coming, that he may put all his enemies under his feet. When they fay, *Make hafte my beloved*, this implies that there was mutual love between them. The foul was made fenfible of Chrift's love to it: " For " we love him, fays the apoftle *John*, be" caufe he firft loved us." And when you have fcripture evidence of his firft loving you, then you can with true faith take up the churches words, and fay, " My beloved " is mine, and I am his." To know that he is yours is the fame thing as to know whatever he has is yours: for by being interefted in him you have a property in all his promifes, graces, and bleffings, in time

and

and in eternity. This is the blessed state of believers; and do you not desire, my brethren, to be in it? is it not happiness indeed to be freed from the fear of death and judgment — nay more, to be able to pray for the coming of Christ, and to love his appearing? What can be more desirable than to know that the almighty judge is your loving Saviour, who when he comes at the last day will make you compleatly blessed both in body and soul? May God put it into all your hearts to desire this, and may he give you faith to pray in the words of the text — " Make haste, my beloved, and be thou like " to a roe or a young hart," — like them in swiftness and speed, for which they are remarkable. It is said of *Asahel* the son of *Zeruiah*, that he was as light of foot as a wild roe; and the *Gadites* who came to *David* at *Ziklag* are celebrated for being as swift as roes upon the mountains. With all this speed would the faithful have Christ to hasten his coming. They had no stronger idea of the greatest speed than what they took from the swiftness of a wild roe, and therefore by this they express the fervent desires of their souls after his speedy coming. He heard their prayers, and he will answer them. He gave them

them many promises in the *Old Testament* of his coming in glory to judge the world, and many more in the *New*. In his last words, with which he shuts up the volume of revelation, he leaves us this sweet and comfortable promise — " Surely I come quickly." Here we have his promise, he will come quickly, and confirmed by a solemn asseveration, surely — and surely, what his truth hath promised, nothing shall be able to hinder his omnipotence from fulfilling: for yet a little while, and he that shall come will come, and will not tarry. And because he seems to tarry, therefore the unbeliever takes occasion to reflect upon the faithfulness of God, and the careless sinner sinks deeper into carnal security; but both these sorts of persons may read their condemnation in the third chapter of the second Epistle of *Peter*, in which he foretells that there should come in the last days scoffers, walking after their own lusts and saying, Where is the promise of his coming? We see no signs of it, for since the fathers fell asleep all things go on as they did from the beginning of the creation. To this the apostle replies, first by saying, it is wilful ignorance to maintain, that the world has suffered no change since the

the creation, for was it not once deſtroyed by a deluge of water? And ſecondly he anſwers, that the Lord is not ſlack concerning his promiſe (as ſome men count ſlackneſs) but is long ſuffering to us ward, not willing that any ſhould periſh, but that all ſhould come to repentance. What theſe men call ſlackneſs is an act of mercy. The judge only waits till the time fixed in the counſel of God be finiſhed, till the number of the elect be perfected, and then ſhall the end come. His delay may ſeem long to us who meaſure time by days and months and years, but with the Lord a thouſand years are but as one day. There is no time in eternity. What ſeems long to us, who are but of yeſterday, is with the Lord ſpeedy: for he that is truth and cannot lie ſays, Surely I come quickly. The longer he has delayed, the ſooner he will come, and therefore my brethren, you ſhould be the more prepared. If you think his delay long, this ſhould haſten you in your preparation, becauſe every moment brings his coming nearer. No one dare affirm that he ſhall not live to ſee the Son of Man coming in the clouds of heaven with power and great glory. If this may be, and every one of us may live to ſee it come to paſs,

pass, Oh what manner of persons ought we to be in all holy conversation and godliness? What diligence should we give to make our calling and election sure? Ought we not to have a clear knowledge of our interest in the judge, and to be assured by faith of his being our Saviour, that we may love his appearing, and pray for it, as the faithful did in the text. They finished their prayer, and closed the book with intreating him to come speedily, and to give them more experience of his love; they desired to have daily more proofs of his being their compleat Saviour, by his acting in each of his anointed offices for them and for their salvation, as their prophet, their priest, and their king. This is I think the meaning of the last words — " Upon the mountains of spices." In our language we apply the word mountain to the highest hills, and we generally fix the idea of barrenness to it. But the scripture applies it to hills, of no great height, and to the most fruitful hills, such as *Carmel*, and *Sharon*, and *Gilead*, upon which grew the spices here mentioned. In the 30th of *Exodus* we have a particular description of these aromatic spices. *Moses* was commanded to take myrrh, cinnamon, sweet calamus, and cassia,

caſſia, and to mix them up with oil olive, to make a compoſition that would diffuſe its fragrant odours without the help of fire. The uſe of this holy ointment was to anoint the tabernacle itſelf, and all its veſſels, that they might be holy unto the Lord — And it was alſo to conſecrate the high prieſt, that he might miniſter in holy things. And it was ſtrictly forbidden in the law to uſe it to any other purpoſe, upon the penalty of death. This holy anointing was to repreſent what was to be in Chriſt, and what was to flow to us from him. It was the type and figure of the anointing of the Holy Spirit, which was poured upon him without meaſure, to conſecrate him to the high offices of prophet prieſt, and king, over the people of God. He is their prophet to enlighten the blindneſs of their underſtanding, and to lead them into all ſaving truth, their prieſt to take away the pollution and guilt of ſin, and their king to deſtroy in them the dominion of ſin, and to carry on the divine life in their ſouls here in grace, and hereafter in glory. The faithful in the *Old Teſtament* expected him in theſe gracious offices, for which he was to be qualified by the unction from the holy one, and therefore they made it a matter of their prayers that he would haften his coming in his three office characters, which they exprefs by that holy anointing, whereby he was conftituted and ordained to thefe offices.

The meaning of the words from what has been faid appears to be this. The faithful finifh this fweet portion of fcripture with a prayer. They had experienced fo much of Chrift's love, that their hearts were entirely fet upon further communion, and therefore they beg of him to haften his coming; in the *Old Teftament* they mean his coming in the flefh, in the *New* we mean his coming to judgment; but both to them and us there is another coming. Chrift muft come and dwell in our hearts by faith, that we may receive the benefits of his firft coming in the flefh and be prepared for his fecond coming in glory: for until we have by faith a clear view of our intereft in him, how can we take up the words of the text and fay — Make hafte, O thou beloved Jefus, and for the elects fake fhorten thefe days of fin and blafphemy. Why is thy chariot fo long in coming? Why tarry the wheels of thy chariot? Oh come with all the fwiftnefs
of

of the fleeteſt roe, or wild deer, to fulfil whatever remains of ſcripture not compleated, eſpecially come to fulfil what is written of the ſacred offices, to which thou waſt anointed, and by which thou art to make us an odour of a ſweet ſmell, a ſacrifice acceptable, well-pleaſing unto God. Thus come, Lord Jeſus, as our prophet and prieſt, and ſet up thy kingdom of grace in every one of our hearts, that we may love thy appearing, and pray thee to haſten thy kingdom of glory.

Upon this ſtate of the doctrine there are two practical truths offered to our ſerious conſideration.

Firſt, The prayer for Chriſt's coming. And

Secondly, The reaſon upon which the prayer was grounded.

And *Firſt*, As to his coming at the laſt day, it is as certain, as that he came in the fleſh in the fulneſs of time. From the certainty of the fact the faithful were led to pray for it. And can you, my brethren, join in their

their prayer? Do you defire from your hearts that Chrift fhould foon come in all his glory to judgment? Are you preparing and looking out for it as an event that may not be far off? If you are, then you are fafe. But if you are not, examine carefully what is the reafon. Why cannot you pray along with the faithful for Chrift's fpeedy coming to judgment? Surely you don't doubt of the fact? That he will come to judge the world is as certain as that he did come at the fixt time to judge the *Jewifh* nation: " For we " muft all appear before the judgment-feat of " Chrift." The matter of fact upon fcripture principles is undeniably clear and certain. Why then are you not fo prepared for it as to make it the fubject of your prayers? Is it becaufe you put it at a great diftance, and therefore think yourfelves fafe? Confider attentively, what the fcripture fays upon this point. Our Lord has given us feveral marks and figns of his coming, by which we might know as certainly, when it was at hand, as we could know, when the fig-tree puts forth her green figs, that fummer is nigh. There were to be wars and rumours of wars, peftilences, earthquakes in divers places, very little truth faith left upon the earth, and yet

as

as great fecurity among carelefs finners as there was in the days of *Noah*, when the flood came and fwept them all away. Do you think thefe cannot be the forerunners of our Lord's fpeedy coming, becaufe there always have been fuch things in the world? But when all thefe figns are at once upon the earth, and in a manner they never were before, then they become loud calls to an immediate preparation. Were there ever greater wars, or more rumours of war? Has not an uncommon peftilence raged among the cattle for feveral years, in this and in other countries? Were there ever fuch earthquakes, fo univerfal, and of fo long continuance, as have been for fome years paft? And does not the prefent ftate of the world as to religion greatly refemble our Lord's defcription of the men, upon whom that day fhall come unawares as a thief in the night? And when could the account which St. *Paul* gives us in feveral of his epiftles, of the men of the latter times be more true, than it is at prefent? Have they not the name and form of chriftianity without the power of it? Are they not worldly-minded, funk into carnal fecurity, and fo entirely influenced by the love of pleafure, that the love of God and

of

of the things of God is not only waxed cold, but quite frozen up? Was there ever any age, wherein our Lord's words could be more strictly fulfilled, " When the Son of " Man cometh shall he find faith upon the " earth?" By these signs our Lord is alarming a sinful world with notices of his speedy coming, and if sinners are not at all alarmed, but continue still secure in their sins, this is a scripture proof that he will soon come as a thief in the night and surprize them: for when they shall say, Peace and safety, then sudden destruction shall come upon them, and they shall not escape.

But still you do not see the signs of his coming so clearly, as to be convinced of the necessity of being immediately prepared. If it be at all necessary to be prepared, it is certainly necessary to be prepared immediately: for you cannot be sure at any time, that he will not come, and therefore you should be at all times ready for his coming. Suppose he should come in a day that ye look not for him, what would your eternal condition be? What, if he should surprize you in your sins, have you no apprehension about your danger? Who amongst you could dwell with

the

the devouring fire? Who amongst you could dwell with the everlasting burnings? And suppose he should not come, yet if he send death to surprize you, it is the same thing. If you die unpardoned you are lost for ever: for it is written, " the wicked shall be " turned into hell, and all the people that " forget God." So that put our Lord's coming as far off as you please, yet you cannot put death off: and there is the same preparation necessary for the one as for the other. You must be turned from darkness to light, and from the power of satan unto God, you must be justified and sanctified, before you are fit either to meet death or judgment. And if you have no knowledge of Christ's being *your* Saviour, it is the same thing to you as if there was no Saviour: for if you are not united by faith to Christ, he is no Christ to you, according to the saying of the first reformers, " That an unapplied Christ " is no Christ;" therefore, my beloved brethren, if you have any real love for your own souls, if you indeed prefer everlasting joys to endless torments, seek for pardon and peace from the hands of Jesus Christ, who has them to give, that having received them from him, you may be able with true faith to use the prayer in the text, and for the same reason the faithful here used it, namely, from your experience of your interest in Christ, which is the *second* practical point in the text I was to apply.

They pray to Christ to hasten his coming; which they earnestly requested, because they had clear evidence of his being *their* loving Saviour. He first loved them, and made them sensible of his love, therefore they loved him. And having a sure interest in the present graces of his salvation (for they were in possession, and had actual enjoyment of them) they knew that they should at his second coming share in the blessings of his eternal kingdom; for which reason they offered up to him the prayer of faith, requesting him to come quickly—Make haste, my beloved, and may we soon see thee manifest in the flesh, making an atonement for sin and bringing in everlasting righteousness, and when thou hast by obeying, suffering, dying, and rising again fulfilled the law and the prophets, Oh hasten thy second coming. Let all things be forwarded that are to go before it. Finish the number of thine elect, *Jews* and *Gentiles*, and then come in the clouds of heaven with

power

power and great glory. Now, my brethren, do you pray thus for Chrift's fecond coming? Can you make it, do you make it, the daily fubject of your prayers? Being affured that Jefus is your Saviour, have you no fear of him as your judge? Are you fo entirely delivered from fear that you love his appearing, as the day of the Lord's great glory, when he will be glorified in the deftruction of all his enemies, and glorified much more in the eternal falvation of all his faints?

Perhaps fome of you may think, that it favours of enthufiafm, for a man to pretend to be fo certain of Chrift's love, as to pray for his coming to judgment. Let us hear then what the fcripture fays. The faithful in the text defire Chrift to make hafte, and upon this motive they ground their prayer, that he was *their beloved*; but they could not have urged him to make hafte for this reafon, unlefs they had been certain of their intereft in him. If he had not been *their beloved*, they could not have made their hopes of meeting him foon the fubject of their prayers; but every one could fay for himfelf, " My beloved is mine and I am his," and knowing that they were his, and belonged

to him, knowing this from the work of grace which was in them, from the abiding witnefs of the Spirit, and from the long and fweet communion which they had enjoyed with their beloved Jefus, they therefore prayed him to make hafte, to haften his firft and fecond coming. And if this be enthufiafm, it is not peculiar to this portion of fcripture. It runs through the whole volume as well as through the fong. All the patriarchs, as well as *Abraham*, defired to fee Chrift's day. *Mofes* prayed earneftly for it, and was honoured with the fight of it, as *Abraham* was; God fhewed it to them in a vifion, but he did not vouchfafe the fame to many prophets and kings and righteous men, although they earneftly defired to fee it. The *Pfalms* and the prophetical writings are full of petitions to Chrift, praying him to come to the falvation of his people. And the *New Teftament* abounds with the like petitions. It is faid of believers that they love their Lord's appearing—they love it and make it the fubject of their prayers, becaufe they know it will be an happy event for them. Daily are they looking up to him, and praying " thy kingdom come," and befeeching him in the words of our church,
" fhortly

" shortly to accomplish the number of his
" elect, and to hasten his kingdom."

Thus it is so far from being enthusiasm to love Christ's appearing, that it is one of the plain truths of scripture, clearly taught and strongly enforced in numerous passages both of the *Old Testament* and of the *New;* and it is a doctrine received by our church, and made use of in her liturgy. And certainly, my brethren, you will not oppose a truth confirmed by so many proofs? This would be acting a very irrational part, and would be a clear sign of your being under great guilt: for it would prove you to be without the least sense of that love which you oppose. If you had ever seen your want of that love, had ever been seeking it, or had ever tasted of it, you could not deny there is such a thing as loving Christ, because he first loved you. This is a received truth in scripture. In the Song it is taken for granted throughout, and in the *New Testament* it is expressly asserted. " We have known, say some, the " love that God hath to us." And another declares, " Jesus Christ loved me, and gave " himself for me." And we may still know this by the very same means, by which they

knew

knew it, *viz.* by the Holy Ghoſt's ſhedding abroad the love of God in our hearts. Until he ſhed it abroad in your hearts you cannot join the faithful in the text, and pray with them for Chriſt's coming, becauſe if you love him not, how can you love his appearing? You cannot call him *your beloved*, and therefore you have no intereſt in him. Conſider and examine whether this be a deſirable ſtate to live in, and to die in. What is it to be without Chriſt? Is it not to be aliens from the commonwealth of *Iſrael*, and ſtrangers from the covenants of promiſe, to have no hope, and to be without God in the world? This is the ſcripture account of your dangerous condition. And does not it alarm you? If it does, fly to Chriſt, and he will give you to taſte of his pardoning love. If it does not, may he ſend his good Spirit to convince you what it is to be without Chriſt, that you may feel the miſery of it in time, and therefore may ſeek to be happy with him in eternity.

If then the ſame ſpirit be in you, which was in the faithful in the text, you will be able to take up their words, and to ſpeak them with their faith. You will have ſuch a clear a clear view of your intereſt in the beloved Jeſus, that the thoughts of his coming ſoon to judgment will be matter of joy and delight, and this will furniſh you with the beſt comment upon the Song. The experience of Chriſt's love makes it plain and eaſy. For he that has this love in his heart will not be much at a loſs to underſtand what is here written of it. He is not like a novice, who begins to learn the firſt principles of ſome art or ſcience, but he is a great proficient. He has been taught of God, and has received a practical and experimental knowledge of the ſubject of this book. It treats of the believers happineſs in being united to Chriſt, and he is united to Chriſt, and finds himſelf happy in that union: for he knows the love which Chriſt has to his ſoul, and he has received many clear ſcripture marks and evidences of it. The Holy Spirit has ſhed abroad the love of Chriſt in his heart, and he loves Chriſt, becauſe he knows Chriſt firſt loved him. He loves God the Father, who is now his reconciled father, and he loves and delights to do his will. He loves the Lord's-day, his ordinances, his people, and in ſhort he loves every thing that God loves. He has indeed in his heart that love

of which this book treats, and his own experience daily opens and explains it so clearly, as if it had been written for his particular use, and was a copy of God's dealings with his soul. He finds that nearness to God, which is here described. He has much sweet communion with him in prayer. In time of temptation, or affliction, he can go boldly to the throne of grace; faith gives him boldness and access with confidence: for he is assured that whatever he asks in his Saviour's name he shall receive. When he hears or reads the word he can mix faith with it, and he is enabled to grow thereby. And when he goes to the Lord's supper, he finds that Christ is still present at his own table, and makes himself known in breaking of bread. He finds a nearness to Christ, and enjoys sweet fellowship with him in all the ordinances. He lives in his presence, is led by his Spirit, and partakes of his comforts. In short he is united to Christ intimately and vitally, as a member of the body is to the head, or as the branches are to the vine, or as the bread is to the eater, or as the building is to the foundation; for under these and several such-like images the scripture describes the
union

union there is between Christ and the believer. Our church speaking of it says, That believers are one with Christ, and he with them, that they dwell in Christ, and Christ in them. Surely then they that are thus closely united to Christ will know the most of this book, and will be the best commentators upon it: for it is not a sealed book to them. The subject-matter is to them plain and open. Daily experience gives them clearer views of its sweetness and fulness, and every step they advance in the divine life affords them fresh occasion to bless and praise God for this comfortable portion of his holy word.

My brethren, if you are united to Christ in the bonds of love, you know that these things are true; but if you have not his love in your heart, nor desire it, you are not fit to read the Song: for you cannot understand it. A deaf man is as good a judge of a fine piece of music, as you are of a treatise upon that love, of which you never had a taste. The Song is a book of experience, describing Christ's love to his people, and the happiness they have in the sense of his love; but if you have no

sense

sense of it, how can you understand what is here written concerning it? If you should take it up and read it, having never had any fellowship with the Father nor the Son by the bond of the Spirit, it will appear to you an unintelligible piece of jargon. The *English* translation would be as dark and mysterious as the original *Hebrew*, which you do not understand: for it is a sealed book, until the Holy Spirit open its meaning; but all becomes plain and clear, when he sheds abroad in the heart that love of which it treats, and the more he gives you to taste of the love of Christ, the plainer and sweeter will the book grow in your esteem.

My christian friends and brethren, you know these things to be true from your own experience. You set a great value upon this sweet portion of scripture, and desire to see the depths and heights of it: they will open more fully to your view, if you pray for more love, and for nearer communion with Christ. And if any of you my brethren, have been prevailed upon to seek for the happy experience of Christ's love, you are ready to join your hearts with mine to pray to him for a blessing on these discourses. And

And as to you who have not been stirred up to seek, you stand in great need of our prayers, and we will offer them up for you. May he that heareth prayer, hear and answer.

We humbly beseech thee, O thou God of love, to bring into the way of truth all those who have erred and are deceived, concerning this portion of thy divine word. Remove all their prejudices. Shew the natural man, the ridiculer, and the unbeliever, that they want the love of which it treats. Convince them, blessed Jesus, that thy love can make them happy, and nothing else can. Let them feel their guilt, and their danger, while the love of earthly and sensual hinders their seeking for thy spiritual and heavenly joys. And may thy good Spirit shed abroad the love of God in the hearts of all those who are seeking it, that they may find this portion of scripture verified in their own souls, and daily fulfilled in their own experience. Oh that we may all know more of the love of God, and taste and see how gracious the Lord is. May we enjoy that fellowship and communion with the Father, and his son Jesus Christ, which will
explain

explain to our underſtandings and apply to our hearts all the comforts of this divine treatiſe. So be it, Lord Jeſus, to the praiſe of the Father, Son, and Holy Spirit, three Perſons in one Jehovah, to whom the church militant and triumphant gives equal honour, and worſhip, and glory, now and for ever. *Amen* and *Amen*.

F I N I S.

www.ingramcontent.com/pod-product-compliance
Lightning Source LLC
Chambersburg PA
CBHW030409230426
43664CB00007BB/804